S0-DUT-941

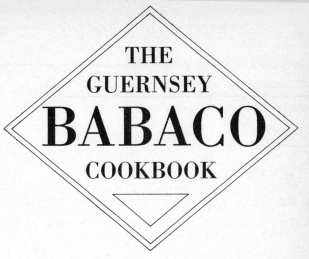

THE GUERNSEY BABACO COOKBOOK

Graham and Sue Edwards

Alan Sutton

CHANNEL ISLAND EXOTICS

1988

Alan Sutton Publishing
Brunswick Road · Gloucester
───────────────────────────
Channel Island Exotics
Guernsey · Channel Islands

First published 1988

Copyright © Graham and Sue Edwards 1988

All rights reserved. No part of this publication may be reproduced, stored in a retrieval
system, or transmitted, in any form or by any means, electronic, mechanical,
photocopying, recording or otherwise, without the prior permission of the publishers
and copyright holder

British Library Cataloguing in Publication Data

Edwards, Graham
   The Guernsey babaco cookbook.
   1. Cookery (Babacos)
   I. Title   II. Edwards, Sue
   641.6'4   B 25

   ISBN 0-86299-499-3

Whilst every care has been taken to ensure that all measurements and details given in
the recipes are correct, the publishers cannot accept any responsibility for inaccuracies
or their consequences.

Cover picture: Left to right: Back – Baked halibut sarnia, A ripe Guernsey babaco,
Babaco fruit salad; Front – Babaco treasure trove, Babaco bordelaise, Babaco and
watercress salad (Photograph: Graham Jackson, Camera Centre, Guernsey). In the
background, a babaco tree with its unripe fruit a dusky blue.

Typesetting and origination by
Alan Sutton Publishing Limited
Photoset 10/11 Times
Printed in Great Britain by
The Guernsey Press Company Limited
Guernsey, Channel Islands

THE
GUERNSEY
BABACO
COOKBOOK

Preface

The saying 'There is nothing new under the sun' became disproved soon after our first finding of the GUERNSEY BABACO. At first, the babaco appeared to be just another fruit that had little to offer other than as an extra ingredient to fruit salads. It was not until we started cooking with the fruit that its full potential emerged. Time after time we found it defied the general laws associated with similar fruits. Especially exciting is the fact that the keeping qualities of the fruit once cut are not impaired, nor is its texture changed when cooked.

The object of this book is to show how versatile the Guernsey babaco really is. The whole range of tried and tested recipes are meant not only as a large set of dishes for cooks to use with the babaco, but also for those adventurous cooks amongst you to experiment with and create new and exciting variations.

The recipes have been compiled using both metric and imperial measures and we have rounded the measurements out to make weighing easier. In doing so, however, the metric recipe will produce slightly less especially if the recipes are multiplied for large numbers. Do not try to mix metric and imperial measurements. We have produced the recipes in the smallest possible quantities to make them suitable for single persons and small families as these groups are often neglected.

The preparation times used throughout the book are based on the average times taken by cooks of various degrees of speed and readers should take this into account when planning their own meals. We have not included any time needed for setting or marinating as this will vary according to the time of the year or individual taste.

Guernsey has an excellent selection of home-produced dairy products, fish and vegetables which are irresistible to the discerning cook and therefore we have used, where possible, fresh produce in the recipes. You may, however, replace these fresh items with substitutes if so required.

The Guernsey babaco is definitely here to stay and we feel it is going to play an important part in our future eating habits.

Graham and Sue Edwards
1988

Contents

Introduction   *ix*
  The Guernsey Babaco   *ix*
  Purchasing   *x*
  Ripening and Storage   *x*
  In the Kitchen   *xi*
  Suggested Wines   *xii*
  Vegetarian Dishes   *xii*
  Nutrition   *xiii*
  Recipe Weights and Measures   *xiv*
  Oven Temperature Scale   *xv*
  Microwave Ovens   *xv*
Breakfast   *1*
Starters   *3*
Fish   *19*
Meat   *38*
Poultry and Game   *55*
Vegetarian Dishes   *65*
Savoury Snacks   *78*
Vegetables   *84*
Salads   *88*
Desserts   *97*
Preserves   *144*
Wines, Liqueurs & Cocktails   *148*
Acknowledgements   *157*
Index   *158*

Introduction

The Guernsey babaco
[*carica pentagona (heilbornii)*]

The Guernsey babaco (pronounced BABA-CO) is a member of the Caricae (paw paw family) and a native fruit of Ecuador, South America. Although Ecuador is on the equator, the babaco likes a humid, sub-tropical environment and grows in the Andean highland forests at an altitude of between 2,000 to 3,000 metres (6,500 to 9,800 feet).

It is a hybrid cross of the *Carica pubescens* (Mountain papaya) and the *Carica stipulata* (Badillo) and was first discovered in 1922 by a German botanist called Heilborn. It was officially classified as a separate species of paw paw in 1929 and has no sub-varieties. In 1975 it was introduced to New Zealand by Dick Endt where it is also grown outdoors in frost-free regions. In 1985 it was introduced into Guernsey by David Miller as part of an experimental project and proved most adaptable to the Guernsey climate.

The babaco tree has a palm-like, truncated appearance with large ornamental leaves growing from the top third of the tree. It grows to a height of 2–3 metres (6–9 feet) in the first year and will produce fruit after nine months. The tree is parthenocarpic (seedless) which means that its flowers do not need pollinating to produce fruit.

The fruit is a fleshed-out carpel with undifferentiated parenchymal tissue and grows on a long stem from each trunk section, ripening from the base upwards. They are marrow-shaped with one end tapering to a point and each of the five sides has a concave edge giving the fruit a star-like shape when sliced across. The tree will bear between 40 and 60 fruits during a full cropping cycle of 15 months. Each fruit averages 30 × 10 centimetres (12 × 4 inches) and weighs between 675 grammes and 1.135 kilogrammes (1½ lbs and 2½ lbs).

The tree has a life-span of 6–10 years and although it produces fruit all the year round in Ecuador, it is seasonal elsewhere. In Guernsey its season starts in late September, peaks in March to May and ends in

July, though the growers are now working towards all-year-round production.

Guernsey's strict plant import control laws mean the Guernsey babaco tree is almost disease-free. The plant is susceptible to botrytis and mildew when grown in the open, but as it is grown under glass in Guernsey and as the use of pesticides is kept to a minimum (using predators to keep insect pests at bay), the Guernsey babaco is a healthy, chemical-free fruit and is, in fact, far superior in skin texture, aroma and flavour to those grown outdoors.

Purchasing

Look for the distinctive 'GUERNSEY BABACO' sticker when purchasing your Guernsey babaco – it guarantees that the fruit is of top quality and has been produced with great care under strict production methods.

The Guernsey babaco is harvested when it is approximately one-third ripe (one-third of its total skin area is yellow, the remainder being deep green). It is then packed in a protective wrapping for retail sale.

On purchasing, the Guernsey babaco should be handled with care as its soft edible skin will bruise easily if knocked.

Ripening and Storage

The Guernsey babaco ripens best at a constant temperature of 20°C to 22°C out of direct sunlight. If purchased with only one-third of the skin surface in a yellow condition this ripening process will take approximately 5–6 days. The fruit will firstly turn a brilliant yellow and then, over the next 24 hours, release a powerful fragrant perfume which signals that it is ready for eating. It is important that the fruit reaches this stage to obtain the full flavour and enjoyment of the babaco.

If the Guernsey babaco is not required for immediate use, storage at a lower temperature will prolong the ripening process (at 12°C the ripening time is doubled). If stored at between 2°C and 6°C (in a domestic refrigerator) the fruit will take 3–4 weeks to ripen if one-third yellow when purchased.

Once ripe, the Guernsey babaco can be cut. The remaining babaco can be either stored cut side down onto a flat surface (ie, a plate), or wrapped in cellophane or kitchen foil and stored in a cool place (6°C –

12°C). Care must be taken if placed in a refrigerator as the babaco's flavour will permeate into such items as milk, cheese, cream, etc. It should therefore be sealed in a polythene bag to prevent any risk of flavour absorbtion. If the end is wrapped with cling-film, the un-used part will keep for up to 5–6 days if stored in a cool place or in the refrigerator, never below 2°C.

The Guernsey babaco is *not* suitable for deep-freezing unless it has been liquidised into a purée or has been cooked as part of a dish.

In the Kitchen

The Guernsey babaco offers an exciting new look to our eating habits, being very versatile, 98 per cent edible and virtually seedless (some of the fruits occasionally have traces of seeds within them but these are always infertile).

As the babaco ripens the high acid content lowers. This enables the cook to use the babaco at various stages of ripeness depending on the recipe.

On cutting a ripe Guernsey babaco, juice will surge from the cut surfaces, but this will be the only juice lost until a further slice is removed (the flesh has a light orange/pink tinge). During the cooking process, unlike many other fruits, the Guernsey babaco retains its shape and will not break up. This allows the chef to use it as a major ingredient, or as a garnish in a wide range of dishes.

The fruit's skin is very tender and easily digested. Many of the recipes require that the babaco need only be sliced; where the recipe calls for the babaco to be puréed then, in most cases, the whole fruit (skin and pulp) is used. When the whole fruit is used in purée form the resulting pulp is a thick homogenous mass and therefore some recipes require the babaco to be either peeled before liquidising or strained through a fine strainer after liquidising. Whichever method is used, if the peel is removed it can be used to flavour stocks, sauces, stews, syrups, etc, or added to a recipe where the purée can contain the peel. Otherwise the peel can be squeezed to remove any juice it contains and added to the recipe. To peel the babaco we have found the best way is to cut it into 2 cm (¾ in) slices and then, using a sharp paring knife, remove the skin in stages.

Once the babaco has reached 100 per cent ripeness and within 5–6 days, it will start to gain a soft appearance and touch. The babaco is perfectly acceptable in this state and ideal for many of the dessert recipes, and for making cocktails and fruit cups.

The Guernsey babaco contains an enzyme called papain which is most beneficial to the cook as it acts as a meat tenderiser and therefore will render tough cuts of meat more digestible than a marinade containing wine. This is especially useful for game and saves the need for long 'hanging' periods.

Babaco juice can be used as an alternative to lemon juice, offering a softer acidity than lemon juice especially when used with delicate fish dishes. It can also replace lemon juice to prevent peeled fruits, such as apples, from turning brown, without making them too acidic.

In its simplest form the Guernsey babaco can be added to fruit salads to give them a superb flavour and aroma or cut into slices and served with a simple dressing of cottage cheese, flavoured herb vinegar or with ice cream. Chilled it is refreshing and thirst quenching.

Suggested Wines

The Guernsey babaco goes well with fruity, medium to dry white wines such as:

German:	Kabinett wines made from the Riesling, Morio Muskat, Müller-Thurgau and Kerner grapes.
Italian:	Soave, Frascati, Orvieto and Pinot Grigio.
French:	Champagne, Alsatian wines, white Loire wines and dry sparkling wines.
Spanish:	White Rioja, Cava wines and dry white Penedés wines.
Portuguese:	White Dão, Vinhos Verdes.

On the whole red wines do not marry well with dishes cooked with the Guernsey babaco. However some light red wines are suitable for drinking with meat dishes containing babaco, for example Beaujolais from France, red Baden wines from Germany and Austrian red wines.

Vegetarian Dishes [V]

The Guernsey babaco offers vegetarians a versatile new ingredient to add to their culinary repertoire. Whilst the babaco is a fruit, it has only a low sugar content, enabling it to be used in both sweet and savoury dishes.

The recipes suitable for vegetarians have been marked **[V]** and contain no meat or fish. They do however contain dairy products, but these can easily be substituted with alternative ingredients to suit the requirements of those following such a diet. The desserts are all suitable as vegetarian dishes and therefore have not been marked with the **[V]**.

Other recipes may also be adapted, omitting or replacing certain unacceptable ingredients e.g. meat stocks with vegetable stocks, meat or fish with textured vegetable protein (soya), butter with vegetarian margarine, etc.

Nutrition

Nutritionally the Guernsey babaco will contribute a great deal to a healthy diet. Low in sugar and fats and with a good vitamin C content, it offers those on a low calorie diet a useful addition to their daily menu.

NUTRITIONAL COMPOSITION

[per 100 grammes (3½ ozs)]

Dietary fibre	0.56 gramme.
Protein	0.74 gramme.
Sugars	8.50 grammes.
Fat	0.60 gramme.
Starch	0.14 gramme.
Vitamin C	0.28 gramme.

This analysis is of a fully ripened Guernsey babaco.

RECIPE WEIGHTS AND MEASURES

Because of the complexity of converting metric into imperial measures and vice-versa (1 ounce equals 28.35 grammes and 1 fluid ounce equals 28.35 mls) and as the recipes in the book are for 1–6 portions, we have simplified matters and worked on the scale as follows:

METRIC	IMPERIAL	SPOON
5 grammes	¼ ounce	1 teaspoon
10 grammes	⅓ ounce	2 teaspoons
15 grammes	½ ounce	1 dessertspoon
20 grammes	¾ ounce	4 teaspoons
25 grammes	1 ounce	2 dessertspoons
50 grammes	2 ounces	
75 grammes	3 ounces	
100 grammes	4 ounces	
200 grammes	8 ounces	
400 grammes	1 pound	

When using the spoon measure a 'spoon' denotes a heaped spoonful.

METRIC	IMPERIAL	SPOON
5 millilitres	¼ fluid ounce	2 teaspoons
10 millilitres	⅓ fluid ounce	3 teaspoons
15 millilitres	½ fluid ounce	2 dessertspoons
20 millilitres	¾ fluid ounce	3 dessertspoons
25 millilitres	1 fluid ounce	4 dessertspoons
50 millilitres	2 fluid ounces	
75 millilitres	3 fluid ounces	
100 millilitres	4 fluid ounces	
200 millilitres	8 fluid ounces	
250 millilitres	½ pint	
500 millilitres	1 pint	

OVEN TEMPERATURE SCALE

GAS MARK	CELCIUS SCALE [°C]	FARENHEIT [°F]
¼	110°C	225°F
½	130°C	250°F
1	140°C	275°F
2	150°C	300°F
3	170°C	325°F
4	180°C	350°F
5	190°C	375°F
6	200°C	400°F
7	220°C	425°F
8	230°C	450°F
9	240°C	475°F

Note

Old style ovens (especially electric) will be marked in the Farenheit temperature scale.

All ovens should be checked regularly to ensure that the thermostat is operating efficiently.

The temperature given for each recipe is for foods placed in the centre of the oven (unless a convection oven is being used).

Recipes suitable for MICROWAVE cooking are marked [**M**].

Microwave Ovens [M]

The Guernsey babaco is ideal for cooking in a microwave oven and will hold its shape during the cooking process, losing none of its nutritional value.

The recipes in this book have been written for preparation on conventional cooking equipment (solid fuel, gas or electric) and those recipes that are suitable for cooking with the aid of a microwave oven have been marked **[M]**.

As there are many styles, sizes and power outputs of microwave ovens on the market it is impossible to give accurate cooking times and therefore those wishing to utilise a microwave oven should follow the manufacturer's instructions.

Most of the recipes marked with the **[M]** symbol will require the use of an open flame to cook sauces (although some microwave ovens do offer this facility) and the use of a top grill, although again many top of the range microwave ovens incorporate a browning facility.

Breakfast

GUERNSEY MUESLI

PREPARATION TIME: *20 minutes*   [V]

Ingredients *(per person)*:

100 g (4 oz) **Guernsey babaco**
50 g (2 oz) rolled oats
1 dessert apple
1 tablespoon clear honey
25 ml (1 fl oz) double cream
15 g (½ oz) soft brown sugar
50 g (2 oz) sultanas
25 g (1 oz) nuts, chopped

Method:

1   Peel the babaco and liquidise the pulp. Squeeze the skin to obtain the juice.
2   Place the rolled oats in a bowl, add the babaco pulp and juice and leave overnight.
3   Dice the apple (with the skin on) and add to the babaco mixture. Add the remaining ingredients, mix well and serve in a glass bowl.

OAT COCKTAIL WITH FRUIT

PREPARATION TIME: *25 minutes*   [V]

Ingredients *(per 2 persons)*:

50 ml (2 fl oz) full cream milk
25 g (1 oz) rolled oats
25 g (1 oz) clear honey

75 ml (3 fl oz) yogurt
20 ml (¾ fl oz) lemon juice
½ medium red (dessert) apple

½ medium green (dessert) apple
25 g (1 oz) hazelnuts
150 g (6 oz) **Guernsey babaco**
50 g (2 oz) blackberries
50 g (2 oz) strawberries
50 g (2 oz) bilberries
2 whole strawberries
2 mint leaves

Method:

1 Warm the milk and add the oats. Allow to stand for 15 minutes.

2 Mix in the honey, yogurt and lemon juice. Grate the apple halves and mix in.

3 Chop the nuts and toast under a salamander (top grill).

4 Cut the babaco into 1 cm (⅓ in) cubes and gently fold into the mixture.

5 Place the fruit in tall cocktail glasses, top with the oatmeal and babaco mixture, dress with a whole fresh strawberry and mint leaf.

Recipe supplied by Ashley A. Huntley

Starters

BABACO AND CARROT SOUP

PREPARATION TIME: *30 minutes*   **COOKING TIME:** *1 hour*   [M]   [V]

Ingredients *(per 4 persons)*:

600 g (1½ lb) carrots
50 g (2 oz) butter
50 g (2 oz) onion, diced
500 ml (1 pt) vegetable stock
1 orange (juice and zest)
200 g (8 oz) **Guernsey babaco**
Salt and milled black pepper
15 ml (½ fl oz) cream
½ teaspoon chives, chopped

Method:

1   Peel and grate the carrots.
2   Melt the butter in a thick pan, add the onion and carrots, cover with a lid and stew over a low heat for 10 minutes. *DO NOT BROWN*.

3   Add the stock, orange juice and zest, bring to the boil and allow to simmer for 30 minutes until vegetables are well cooked.
4   Liquidise the babaco and add to the soup. Bring back to the boil and simmer for a further 10 minutes.
5   Liquidise, return to the boil, correct consistency with a little more stock if required. Season with salt and pepper. Add cream and chives and serve with garlic bread.

Note: Chicken stock can be used in place of the vegetable stock.

BABACO AND HERB SOUP

PREPARATION TIME: *1 hour*   [V]

Ingredients *(per 2 persons)*:

300 g (12 oz) **Guernsey babaco**
1 medium onion
2 cloves garlic
50 g (2 oz) cucumber
1 small green pepper
1 small red pepper
25 ml (1 fl oz) olive oil
25 ml (1 fl oz) lemon juice
½ teaspoon parsley, chopped
½ teaspoon tarragon, chopped
½ teaspoon thyme, chopped
Salt and milled white pepper
100 ml (4 fl oz) iced water
4 ice cubes
25 g (1 oz) white breadcrumbs

Method:

1   Peel the babaco and liquidise the flesh. Squeeze the skin and save the juice. Mix together and chill.
2   Finely chop the onion, garlic, cucumber and peppers, place into a tureen with the oil, lemon juice and chopped herbs and stand in a cool place for 1 hour.
3   Mix the babaco with the vegetables, season, add iced water and 4 ice cubes.
4   Serve with breadcrumbs (served separately in a sauceboat).

BABACO BISQUE

PREPARATION TIME: *20 minutes*   COOKING TIME: *30 minutes*

Ingredients *(per 2 persons)*:

150 g (6 oz) **Guernsey babaco**
50 g (2 oz) peeled prawns
25 g (1 oz) butter
25 g (1 oz) plain flour
1 clove garlic, minced
25 g (1 oz) shallots, finely diced
50 ml (2 fl oz) Muscadet (or
    other dry white wine).

500 ml (1 pt) fish stock
15 ml (½ fl oz) cream
½ teaspoon parsley, chopped

Method:

1   Peel the babaco and cut into 1 cm (⅓ in) cubes. Squeeze the peel and save any juices.

2 Roughly chop the prawns.

3 Fry the garlic and shallots in the butter, add the prawns and cook over a low heat for 2 minutes. Add the flour and cook for a further 2 minutes.

4 Add the wine, babaco juices and fish stock (see recipe GUERNSEY BABACO FISH CHOWDER) a little at a time, stirring constantly. Bring to the boil and simmer for 20 minutes.

5 Add the babaco cubes, simmer for a further 5 minutes.

6 Correct the seasoning, add cream and chopped parsley and serve.

Note: Other shellfish (crab, lobster, shrimps, etc.) can be used in place of or with the prawns.

BABACO BAKED EGG ITALIENNE

PREPARATION TIME: *15 minutes*   **COOKING TIME:** *10 minutes*   **[V]**

Ingredients *(per person)*:

1 slice 2.5 cm (1 in) **Guernsey babaco**
1 (size 2) egg
15 g (½ oz) butter
15 g (½ oz) tomato purée
25 ml (1 fl oz) cream
25 g (1 oz) breadcrumbs
15 g (½ oz) parmesan cheese
¼ teaspoon oregano, chopped
Salt and milled black pepper

Method:

1 Butter a *sur le plat* dish (or other small suitable flat ovenproof dish).

2 Remove and discard the centre pulp from the babaco, slice and place in the dish. Save some of the juice.

3 Soft boil the egg, allow to cool, then remove the shell carefully. Place egg into the centre of the babaco.

4 Blend the tomato purée, cream, parmesan cheese, breadcrumbs and seasoning in a liquidiser (adding a teaspoon of babaco juice). Fold in the chopped oregano.

5 Pour the sauce over the egg and babaco and bake in an oven at 200°C (gas mark 6) for 10 minutes.

BABACO EGG TIMBALE

PREPARATION TIME: *30 minutes*   **COOKING TIME:** *45 minutes*   [V]

Ingredients *(per 4 persons)*:

200 g (8 oz) **Guernsey babaco**
3 (size 2) eggs
Salt and milled white pepper
1 kiwi fruit
50 ml (2 fl oz) Muscadet (or
    other dry white wine)
3 sheets leaf gelatine or 5 g (¼
    oz) powdered gelatine
1 sprig dill/tomato rose

Method:

1 Peel the babaco and liquidise
with the eggs. Strain, season
with salt and pepper to taste.
2 Lightly oil 4 dariole moulds
and fill with the babaco mixture.
Place moulds in a pan of hot
water (*bain-marie*), cover with a
sheet of kitchen foil and cook in
an oven at 150°C (gas mark 2)
for 30–40 minutes until set.
3 Remove from the *bain-marie*,
allow to cool and place in a
refrigerator for 2 hours.
4 Peel the kiwi fruit and
liquidise with the wine. Heat
gently, add the gelatine (which
has been soaked in cold water
until soft) and dissolve.
5 Pour the kiwi jelly into the
well of the serving plates and
allow to set in a cold place.
6 To serve: remove the babaco
eggs from the dariole moulds by
tapping gently to loosen and
then turn out onto the centre of
the kiwi jelly.
7 Decorate with a sprig of
fresh dill (or a tomato rose).

Recipe supplied by Roger Goodlass

SPICY BABACO EGGS

PREPARATION TIME: *45 minutes*   **COOKING TIME:** *40 minutes*   **[V]**

Ingredients *(per 2 persons)*:

3 (size 3) eggs
25 g (1 oz) butter
25 g (1 oz) plain flour
100 ml (4 fl oz) milk
25 g (1 oz) onion, diced
1 clove garlic, diced
1 teaspoon parsley, chopped
Salt and milled black pepper
25 g (1 oz) rolled oats
50 g (2 oz) white breadcrumbs
50 g (2 oz) seasoned flour
Sauce:
100 g (4 oz) **Guernsey babaco**
25 g (1 oz) onion, diced
1 clove garlic, diced
25 g (1 oz) butter (or oil)
10 g (⅓ oz) curry powder
15 g (½ oz) plain flour
½ teaspoon tomato purée

Method:

1 Hard boil 2 of the eggs. Melt the butter, add the flour and cook for 2 minutes over a low heat until it has the appearance of wet sand. Add the heated milk a little at a time stirring well until it has all been absorbed. Fry the diced onions and garlic and add to mix. Grate the eggs, add to the mix with the parsley, salt and pepper. Cool in the refrigerator.
2 Mix the rolled oats with the breadcrumbs, beat the remaining egg and then shape the cold egg mixture into cylinders of 6 cm (2½ in) long by 3 cm (1 in) in diameter. Roll in the seasoned flour, then in the beaten egg and finally in the breadcrumb and oat mixture. Deep fry in hot fat (175°C) until crisp and brown.
3 For the sauce: peel and liquidise the babaco flesh. Fry the onion and diced garlic in the butter, add the curry powder and flour and cook for 2 minutes, add the tomato purée and cook for a further minute. Next add the babaco pulp and juices a little at a time, reboiling after each addition. Simmer for 20 minutes, adding a little water if too thick. Serve with the hot egg croquettes.

BABACO AND MUSSEL SALAD

PREPARATION TIME: *20 minutes*

Ingredients *(per 2 persons)*:

100 g (4 oz) **Guernsey babaco**
1 medium tomato, skinned and
   depipped
25 ml (1 fl oz) cream
15 ml (½ fl oz) wine vinegar
15 ml (½ fl oz) olive oil
Salt and milled black pepper
1 teaspoon tarragon, shredded
200 g (8 oz) mussels, cooked
   and shelled
25 g (1 oz) shallots, finely
   chopped

Method:

1 Cut the babaco in half and slice into thin 0.5 cm (¼ in) slices.
2 Finely dice the tomato.
3 Blend the cream, vinegar, olive oil, salt and pepper, then mix in the tarragon to make the dressing.
4 Place the babaco, mussels, tomato and chopped shallots into a bowl, add the dressing and mix lightly.
5 Serve on salad dishes with buttered brown bread.

BABACO HORS D'OEUVRES

PREPARATION TIME: *30 minutes*

Ingredients *(per 4 persons)*:

400 g (1 lb) **Guernsey babaco**
50 g (2 oz) parma ham
25 g (1 oz) smoked oysters
50 g (2 oz) Cheddar cheese
50 g (2 oz) blue vein cheese.
50 g (2 oz) cucumber
½ green pepper
½ red pepper
6 cherry tomatoes
6 stuffed olives

Method:

1 Cut the babaco into 2 cm (¾ in) cubes.
2 Cut the remaining ingredients into 2 cm (¾ in) cubes where possible.
3 Wrap some of the babaco cubes in thin slices of parma ham.
4 Skin the cherry tomatoes (plunge into boiling water for 10

seconds then into cold water, and remove the skin with a sharp knife).

5 Using cocktail sticks, impale assorted cubes of food with the babaco, i.e. babaco, smoked oyster and olive, babaco wrapped in parma ham, cucumber and olive, babaco, blue cheese and red pepper, babaco, cherry tomato and cheddar cheese, etc.

CAVIAR-STUFFED BABACO

PREPARATION TIME: *20 minutes*

Ingredients *(per 2 persons)*:

2 × 2.5 cm (1 in) slices
  Guernsey babaco
25 g (1 oz) caviar
25 g (1 oz) shallots
½ teaspoon parsley, chopped
50 ml (2 fl oz) soured cream
  (Smétane)
1 pinch paprika pepper
½ a lemon
4 slices wholemeal bread

Method:

1 Place the babaco slice on a fish plate and chill.

2 Remove the soft centre pulp and fill the cavity with the caviar [or lumpfish roe].

3 Decorate the plate with a line of finely chopped shallots and finely chopped parsley.

4 Prior to serving coat with the soured cream (Smétane) and a sprinkling of paprika pepper.

5 Serve with a wedge of lemon (with the core and pips removed) and wholemeal melba toast (place thin slices of bread on a baking tray in a cool oven, 150°C (gas mark 2), for approximately 1 hour, until dry and crisp).

COCKTAIL BABACO FRUITS DE MER

PREPARATION TIME: *15 minutes*

Ingredients *(per person)*:

50 g (2 oz) **Guernsey babaco**
50 g (2 oz) shellfish
15 g (½ oz) lettuce, shredded
15 g (½ oz) tomato flesh (diced)
1 pinch paprika pepper
Vinaigrette:
2 teaspoons olive oil
1 teaspoon malt vinegar
Salt and milled black pepper
Dressing:
1 teaspoon **babaco** juice
1 teaspoon tomato purée
25 ml (1 fl oz) mayonnaise
1 dash Tabasco sauce.

Method:

1 Peel the babaco and dice into small cubes. Mix with the shellfish.
2 Blend the babaco juice, tomato purée and mayonnaise together. Add a dash of Tabasco to taste.
3 Place the shredded lettuce in the base of a suitable glass or dish and place the tomato flesh on top. Coat with the vinaigrette (ingredients mixed well together).
4 Place the babaco and shellfish mixture on top and coat with the mayonnaise dressing.
5 Dress with a piece of thinly sliced babaco and dust with paprika pepper.

Note: The cocktail can be made from just one sort of shellfish (prawns, shrimps, crab, lobster, etc.) if so desired.

MARINATED EEL

PREPARATION TIME: *30 minutes*   **COOKING TIME:** *20 minutes*   **[M]**

Ingredients *(per 4 persons)*:

200 g (8 oz) **Guernsey babaco**
100 ml (4 fl oz) olive oil
2 cloves garlic, diced

300 g (12 oz) onions, sliced
12 peppercorns (black)
2 sprigs rosemary

1 large bayleaf
100 ml (4 fl oz) white wine
   vinegar
800 g (2 lb) freshwater eels
50 g (2 oz) seasoned flour

Method:

1 Liquidise the babaco and
pass through a fine sieve.
2 Heat half the oil and fry the
garlic and onions until soft (not
coloured). Add the peppercorns
and herbs, cook for 2–3 minutes.
3 Add the vinegar and babaco

purée, bring to the boil and
simmer for 15 minutes.
4 Meanwhile: skin and clean
the eel. Cut into 8 cm (3 in)
pieces, roll in the seasoned flour
and fry in the remaining oil for
approximately 10 minutes until
cooked. Drain and place in a
deep serving dish.
5 Cover the eel with the onion
and babaco marinade, allow to
cool and store in a refrigerator
for 12 hours.
6 Serve with crispy French
bread.

HAM CORNETS

PREPARATION TIME: *15 minutes*   COOKING TIME: *10 minutes*   **[M]**

Ingredients *(per 4 persons)*:

150 g (6 oz) **Guernsey babaco**
100 g (4 oz) celery
5 g (¼ oz) English mustard
   powder
50 g (2 oz) plain yogurt
100 g (4 oz) parma ham
Salt and milled black pepper
1 sprig parsley

Method:

1 Cut the babaco into 0.5 cm
(¼ in) cubes.
2 Cut the celery across the
stem to produce thin slices.

Cover with water, season with
salt, bring to the boil and
simmer until cooked (but still
firm). Drain well.
3 Blend the mustard with the
yogurt and add to the celery.
4 Cut the ham into thin slices
and then into semi-circles 8 cm
(3 in) in diameter. Lightly butter
one of the edges and form into a
cone. Any ham trimmings can
be diced and added to the
babaco.
5 Season the babaco with
freshly milled black pepper and
spoon into the cornets.

6 Heap the celery mixture into the middle of a serving dish and make a large well in the centre. Neatly place the cornets along the inside so that the open end is facing outwards. Decorate with a sprig of parsley and serve.

GUERNSEY PLATTER

PREPARATION TIME: *30 minutes* **[V]**

Ingredients *(per 4 persons)*:

400 g (1 lb) **Guernsey babaco**
25 g (1 oz) walnuts
100 g (4 oz) cottage cheese
¼ teaspoon cayenne pepper
2 large kiwi fruit
12 cherry tomatoes, skinned
25 ml (1 fl oz) olive oil
15 ml (½ fl oz) tarragon vinegar
Salt and milled white pepper
1 teaspoon parsley, chopped

Method:

1 Cut the babaco in half and then into thin 5 mm (⅓ in) slices. Lay the slices in a fan design on a round serving plate.
2 Chop the walnuts into small pieces and blend with the cottage cheese and cayenne pepper. Place the cheese into the centre of the babaco and flatten slightly.
3 Peel and thinly slice the kiwi fruit and lay the slices over the cottage cheese.
4 Heap the tomatoes into the centre of the dish to make a neat pile.
5 Whisk the oil and vinegar together, season with salt and pepper, add the parsley and spread over the dish prior to serving.
6 Serve with melba toast (See CAVIAR-STUFFED BABACO).

Note: Paté may be used in place of the cottage cheese and other herb vinegars in place of the tarragon vinegar.

SARK SALAD

PREPARATION TIME: *20 minutes*

Ingredients *(per 4 persons)*:

1 small lettuce
300 g (12 oz) **Guernsey babaco**
2 medium oranges
200 g (8 oz) crabmeat
Dressing:
100 ml (4 fl oz) mayonnaise
50 ml (2 fl oz) soured cream
  (Smétane)
1 teaspoon chives, chopped
½ teaspoon parsley, chopped
15 ml (½ fl oz) anchovy essence
1 teaspoon lemon juice
1 clove garlic, crushed
25 ml (1 fl oz) wine vinegar
Salt and milled black pepper

Method:

1 Mix all the dressing
ingredients together and chill in
the refrigerator.
2 Wash the lettuce, shred
finely and mix with a little of the
dressing.
3 Cut the babaco crossways
into 4 rings.
4 Peel the oranges and cut out
the segments from between the
membrane.
5 Mix the crabmeat and orange
segments together.
6 To serve: place the lettuce
on a salad plate and top with a
babaco ring. Fill the babaco
centre with the crabmeat and
orange, top with a little
dressing.
7 Serve the remaining dressing
in a sauceboat.

WESTWOOD BABACO

PREPARATION TIME: *10 minutes* COOKING TIME: *5 minutes*

Ingredients *(per person)*:

100 g (4 oz) **Guernsey babaco**
1 small clove garlic
15 ml (½ fl oz) olive oil
Salt and milled black pepper

¼ teaspoon English mustard
  powder
1 teaspoon lemon juice
15 ml (½ fl oz) **babaco** juice

½ teaspoon parsley, chopped
25 g (1 oz) smoked bacon
1 tomato, skinned and depipped
25 g (1 oz) cucumber, peeled
25 g (1 oz) peeled prawns
1 small shallot, finely chopped

Method:

1   Slice the babaco thinly and lay in a circle (overlapping) on a suitable plate.
2   Blend the garlic, oil, salt and pepper, mustard, lemon juice and babaco juice together in a liquidiser. Mix in the chopped parsley.
3   Cut the bacon into short thin strips and fry until crisp.
4   Cut the tomato and cucumber into short strips (the same size as the prawns) then mix together with the prawns, bacon and shallots.
5   Heap the prawn mixture onto the sliced babaco and coat with the oil and babaco juice dressing. Serve with melba toast.

BABACO IN TARRAGON CREAM

PREPARATION TIME: *10 minutes*   [V]

Ingredients *(per 2 persons)*:

200 g (8 oz) **Guernsey babaco**
125 ml (¼ pt) double cream
25 ml (1 fl oz) tarragon vinegar
10 g (⅓ oz) castor sugar
Salt and milled black pepper
½ teaspoon fresh tarragon, shredded

Method:

1   Cut the babaco in half and then into slices 1 cm (⅓ in) thick.
2   Lay the babaco slices on a medium sized plate.
3   Beat the cream and tarragon vinegar together until thick (but not stiff). Add the sugar, salt and freshly milled black pepper.
4   Spoon the cream over the sliced babaco and decorate with the shredded fresh tarragon leaves.

BABACO WITH BLUE CHEESE DRESSING

PREPARATION TIME: *15 minutes* [V]

Ingredients *(per 2 persons)*:

1 egg yolk
¼ teaspoon English mustard
  powder
½ teaspoon malt vinegar
Salt and milled black pepper
100 ml (4 fl oz) olive oil
100 g (4 oz) blue vein cheese
50 ml (2 fl oz) mayonnaise
200 g (8 oz) **Guernsey babaco**
2–3 lettuce leaves
15 g (½ oz) chives, chopped

Method:

1 Place the egg yolk, mustard,
vinegar, salt and pepper in a
bowl, whisk together. Add the
oil a little at a time, whilst
whisking continuously until all
the oil is absorbed.
2 Mash the cheese with a fork
and combine with the
mayonnaise.
3 Cut the babaco in half
lengthways and then into 1 cm
(⅓ in) slices.
4 Wash the lettuce and shred
finely. Place on a serving dish.
5 Lay the babaco slices along
the lettuce and coat with the
cheese dressing. Sprinkle with
the chopped chives and serve.

CORN-ON-THE-COB WITH BABACO DRESSING

PREPARATION TIME: *20 minutes*   **COOKING TIME:** *20 minutes*   [M] [V]

Ingredients *(per 2 persons)*:

100 g (4 oz) **Guernsey babaco**
2 hard-boiled egg yolks
2 whole maize cobs
Salt

50 g (2 oz) butter
1 teaspoon parsley, chopped

Method:

1   Peel the babaco and liquidise the flesh. Squeeze the skin and save the juice.
2   Bring the babaco juice to the boil and simmer to reduce the volume by half.
3   Sieve the egg yolks.
4   Place the peeled and trimmed maize cobs in plenty of boiling salted water and simmer for 10–12 minutes until tender. Remove and drain well
5   Place the butter, sieved egg yolks and parsley into the babaco juice. Bring to the boil.
6   Put the maize cobs under the salamander (top grill), brush with the babaco mixture and grill until golden brown.
7   Serve with the remaining hot babaco dressing.

Note: Other herbs may be substituted for the chopped parsley such as thyme, chervil, sage, dill, tarragon, etc.

COUPE BABACO À LA MENTHE

PREPARATION TIME: *10 minutes*   [V]

Ingredients *(per person)*:

150 g (6 oz) **Guernsey babaco**
25 ml (1 fl oz) Champagne (brut)
½ an egg white
25 g (1 oz) castor sugar
2 drops green food colouring
1 scoop lemon water ice
25 ml (1 fl oz) green Crème de Menthe
3 mint leaves

Method:

1   Cut the babaco in half and slice thinly, saving any juices.
2   Blend the Champagne and babaco juices together and pour over the babaco slices.
3   Prepare a Champagne saucer by dipping the rim in a little egg white and then into green-coloured castor sugar (a few drops of green food colouring stirred into castor sugar 1 drop at a time).
4   To serve: place the scoop of lemon water ice into the Champagne saucer and pour the Crème de Menthe over the water ice.

5 Dress the babaco slices in a fan over the water ice, add the juices last.
6 Decorate with the mint leaves that have been frosted (dipped in egg white and castor sugar).

Note: A dry/sweet sparkling wine may be substituted for the Champagne.

This dish may also be served as a sorbet or as a sweet.

DEVILLED BABACO

PREPARATION TIME: *20 minutes*   [V]

Ingredients *(per 2 persons)*:

200 g (8 oz) **Guernsey babaco**
15 g (½ oz) fresh ginger
1 small red chilli pepper
15 g (½ oz) soft brown sugar
1 clove garlic, finely chopped
Salt and milled black pepper
25 ml (1 fl oz) wine vinegar
1 teaspoon chives, chopped

Method:

1 Cut the babaco in half and then into 1 cm (⅓ in) slices.

2 Pound the ginger, chilli, sugar and garlic together with the milled pepper and a little salt.
3 Add the vinegar and allow to marinate for 1 hour.
4 Strain and pour over the babaco. Marinate for 2–3 hours.
5 Remove the babaco, lay neatly on a serving dish, coat with the marinade and sprinkle with the chives.

TANGY ISLAND SURPRISE

PREPARATION TIME: *20 minutes*   [V]

Ingredients *(per 2 persons)*:

1 medium grapefruit
1 medium orange
150 g (6 oz) **Guernsey babaco**

10 ml (⅓ fl oz) Calvados
15 g (½ oz) demerara sugar
2 maraschino cherries

2 mint leaves
½ an egg white
25 g (1 oz) castor sugar

Method:

1 Peel and de-pith the grapefruit and orange and cut out the segments (excluding any membrane). Save any juice.

2 Peel the babaco and cut into pieces the same size as the citrus fruit. Squeeze the peel and save any juice.

3 Place the citrus and babaco juices together, add the Calvados and sugar, and stir until sugar is dissolved.

4 Mix the fruits together, add the juices and place in the refrigerator to chill (2–3 hours).

5 To serve: place into coupe dishes, decorate each with a maraschino cherry and frosted mint leaf (dipped in egg white and castor sugar).

Recipe supplied by Valerie L. Bowles

Fish

BABACO FISH BAKE

PREPARATION TIME: *15 minutes*   **COOKING TIME:** *15 minutes*   **[M]**

Ingredients *(per person)*:

150 g (6 oz) cod fillet (or other
   white fish)
25 g (1 oz) wholemeal flour
15 g (½ oz) rolled oats
½ teaspoon English mustard
   powder
½ teaspoon parsley, chopped
Salt and milled white pepper
50 g (2 oz) butter
50 g (2 oz) **Guernsey babaco**

Method:

1   Skin the cod fillet and
remove any bones.
2   Mix the flour, rolled oats,
mustard, parsley, salt and
pepper together.

3   Melt the butter, dip the cod
fillet in the melted butter and
then into the flour mixture.
Place into a buttered, ovenproof dish. Coat with the
remaining melted butter.
4   Thinly slice the babaco (in
half slices).
5   Bake the fish in a hot oven
200°C (gas mark 6) for 10
minutes. Remove from the oven
and place the babaco slices on
top of the fillet. Brush with a
little melted butter from the dish
and return to the oven for a
further 5 minutes.
6   Serve with minted new
potatoes.

FISH IN BABACO AND GREEN HERB SAUCE

PREPARATION TIME: *30 minutes*   **COOKING TIME:** *30 minutes*   [M]

Ingredients *(per 2 persons)*:

150 g (6 oz) **Guernsey babaco**
200 g (8 oz) spinach
50 g (2 oz) butter
1 teaspoon tarragon, chopped
1 teaspoon parsley, chopped
1 teaspoon sage, chopped
1 teaspoon chervil, chopped
300 g (12 oz) white fish fillet
    (monkfish, gurnard, turbot,
    eels, etc.)
50 g (2 oz) seasoned flour
100 ml (4 fl oz) Muscadet (or
    other dry white wine)
3 egg yolks
Salt and milled black pepper

Method:

1   Liquidise the babaco and pass through a fine sieve.
2   Remove the central vein from the spinach leaves and discard. Shred the leaves into small pieces.
3   Melt the butter over a low heat and sauté the spinach and herbs for 5 minutes.
4   Cut the fish fillet into 5 cm (2 in) pieces, dip in the seasoned flour and add to the herbs. Cook over a low flame for 2–3 minutes.
5   Add the wine and babaco purée, bring to the boil and simmer for 5–6 minutes until fish is cooked.
6   Place the fish in a serving dish.
7   Whisk the egg yolks with 25 ml (1 fl oz) of the cooking liquid and add to the remaining cooking liquid. Whisk over a low flame until it thickens. *DO NOT BOIL*. Correct seasoning. Pour over the fish and serve (hot or cold).

GUERNSEY BABACO FISH CHOWDER

PREPARATION TIME: *45 minutes*   **COOKING TIME:** *45 minutes*   **[M]**

Ingredients *(per 4 persons)*:

25 g (1 oz) butter
400 g (1 lb) white fish bones
1 large bayleaf
2 parsley stalks
750 ml (1½ pt) water
200 g (8 oz) **Guernsey babaco**
2 medium tomatoes
100 g (4 oz) smoked streaky
  bacon
1 clove garlic
¼ teaspoon fresh thyme,
  chopped
50 g (2 oz) onions, diced
50 g (2 oz) green pepper, diced
50 g (2 oz) celery, diced
25 g (1 oz) tomato purée
200 g (8 oz) firm white fish (see
  note)
Salt and milled white pepper
25 ml (1 fl oz) dry sherry
2 thick slices white bread

Method:

1 Butter a saucepan, cut up the
fish bones and place in the pan
together with the bayleaf and
parsley stalks. Cover with the
water, bring to the boil and
simmer for 20 minutes. Strain
and squeeze out the bones to
extract all the juices.

2 Peel and cut the babaco into
small 1 cm (⅓ in) cubes,
squeeze the skins and save any
juice. Skin and de-pip the
tomatoes and dice.

3 Mince the bacon to a fine
purée with the garlic. Mix in the
finely-chopped thyme and shape
into pea-sized balls.

4 In a thick-bottomed pan heat
15 g (½ oz) of butter and fry the
onions, peppers and celery until
soft. Add the tomato purée and
cook for 1 minute.

5 Add the fish stock, bring to
the boil and simmer for 5
minutes. Add the diced fish,
babaco and tomatoes, season
and simmer for a further 5
minutes.

6 To serve: place the bacon
purée balls in a tureen with the
sherry, pour the chowder on top
and serve with cubes of toasted
bread.

Note: Firm fleshed fish such as
monkfish, gurnard, cod and rock
salmon are most suitable.

POISSON LA RAMÉE

PREPARATION TIME: *20 minutes*   **COOKING TIME:** *25 minutes*   **[M]**

Ingredients *(per person)*:

25 g (1 oz) butter
25 g (1 oz) plain flour
150 ml (6 fl oz) fish stock
Salt and milled white pepper
150 g (6 oz) white fish fillet
50 g (2 oz) **Guernsey babaco**
50 ml (2 fl oz) Muscadet (or
   other dry white wine)
15 ml (½ fl oz) double cream
1 egg yolk
¼ teaspoon parsley, chopped

Method:

1   Melt the butter, add the flour
and cook for 2 minutes. Add
100 ml (4 fl oz) of the fish stock
a little at a time to produce a
fish velouté. Cook for 15–20
minutes.
2   Butter a suitable dish, season
with salt and pepper and lay the
skinned fish fillet in the dish.

Place thin slices of babaco along
the top of the fillet, add the
remaining fish stock and white
wine with any babaco juices
released when slicing the fruit.
Cover with a buttered piece of
greaseproof paper and cook in a
moderate oven 180°C (gas
mark 4) for 15 minutes.
3   When cooked, remove fillet
from dish and keep warm. Add
the cooking liquid to the
velouté, bring to the boil,
correct the consistency and
seasoning.
4   Mix cream and egg yolk
together and add to very hot
velouté. *DO NOT REBOIL.*
Add parsley.
5   To serve: spoon a little sauce
onto a serving plate, place fish
fillet on top, coat with the
remaining sauce and glaze under
the grill.

CONGRE GRANDES ROCQUES

PREPARATION TIME: *30 minutes*   **COOKING TIME:** *1½ hours*   **[M]**

Ingredients *(per 4 persons)*:

1.2 kg (3 lb) conger eel
250 ml (½ pt) water
1 small bayleaf
25 g (1 oz) butter
25 g (1 oz) plain flour
250 ml (½ pt) full cream milk
600 g (1½ lb) **Guernsey babaco**
½ teaspoon parsley, finely
  chopped
15 g (½ oz) breadcrumbs

Method:

1 Place the conger piece into a pan, cover with the water, add bayleaf, cover, bring to the boil and simmer for 45 minutes.
2 Remove the eel, allow to cool and cut or flake into pieces. Retain the liquid.
3 Melt the butter in a saucepan, add the flour and cook over a low flame until it has the appearance of wet sand. Add the eel stock a little at a time, stirring well after each addition. Add the hot milk, bring to the boil (stirring continuously) and simmer for 20 minutes. Check seasoning.
4 Cut the babaco in half lengthways (saving the centre pulp and ends for the sauce) and cut into 1 cm (⅓ in) slices. Liquidise the ends and pulp and add to the sauce.
5 Place layers of conger eel and babaco slices into an oven-proof dish and coat with the sauce (to which has been added the chopped parsley).
6 Sprinkle the top with the breadcrumbs and bake in a hot oven at 200°C (gas mark 6) for 15 minutes.
7 Serve immediately.

Recipe supplied by Edith Carey

BAKED BABACO WITH CRAB

PREPARATION TIME: *20 minutes*   **COOKING TIME:** *30 minutes*   **[M]**

Ingredients *(per 4 persons)*:

400 g (1 lb) **Guernsey babaco**
25 g (1 oz) shallots, finely
   chopped
25 g (1 oz) butter
10 g (⅓ oz) mild curry powder
100 ml (4 fl oz) béchamel sauce
Salt and milled black pepper
200 g (8 oz) crab meat
1 teaspoon parmesan cheese
1 tablespoon breadcrumbs
½ teaspoon parsley, chopped

Method:

1   Cut the babaco in half to
produce a 'boat'. Remove the
soft centre.

2   Fry the shallots in the butter
add the curry powder and cook
for 2 minutes over a low flame,
stirring all the time.
3   Add the béchamel sauce,
bring to the boil and season with
salt and pepper.
4   Place the crab in the centre
cavity of the babaco. Coat with
the sauce, sprinkle with the
cheese and breadcrumbs mixed
together and bake in an oven
180°C (gas mark 4) for 20
minutes until topping is crisp
and brown.
5   Sprinkle with chopped
parsley and serve.

FROGS' LEGS WITH BABACO SAUCE

PREPARATION TIME: *20 minutes*   **COOKING TIME:** *10 minutes*   **[M]**

Ingredients *(per person)*:

100 g (4 oz) **Guernsey babaco**
1 clove garlic, chopped
3 pairs frogs' legs

50 g (2 oz) seasoned flour
15 ml (½ fl oz) olive oil
15 g (½ oz) butter

24

25 ml (1 fl oz) dry sherry
25 ml (1 fl oz) cream
½ teaspoon parsley, finely
  chopped

Method:

1 Liquidise the babaco and
garlic.
2 Pass the frogs' legs through
the seasoned flour, shake off the
excess flour.

3 Heat the oil and butter in a
pan over a medium flame and
fry the frogs' legs until brown
and cooked.
4 Remove the legs and keep
warm.
5 De-glaze the pan with the
sherry and babaco juice and
reduce until sauce thickens. Add
the cream and return the frogs'
legs to the sauce.
6 Reboil, add the chopped
parsley and serve.

BAKED HALIBUT SARNIA

PREPARATION TIME: *15 minutes*   **COOKING TIME:** *40 minutes*   **[M]**

Ingredients *(per 2 persons)*:

400 g (1 lb) halibut (or other
  white fish)
25 g (1 oz) butter
150 g (6 oz) **Guernsey babaco**
2 medium tomatoes
50 g (2 oz) streaky bacon
  (smoked)
25 g (1 oz) shallots, diced
15 g (½ oz) plain flour
25 ml (1 fl oz) Muscadet (or
  other dry white wine)
1 bayleaf
Salt and milled white pepper
½ teaspoon parsley, chopped

Method:

1 Cut the fish into 2 pieces and

place in a buttered ovenproof
dish.
2 Cut the babaco into 1 cm
(⅓ in) cubes.
3 Skin, de-pip and cut the
tomato into 1 cm (⅓ in) cubes.
4 Dice the bacon and fry in the
butter with the shallots (do not
brown). Add the flour, cook for
1 minute, add the wine, babaco,
tomato, bayleaf and seasonings,
pour over the fish.
5 Cover with kitchen foil and
bake in an oven at 170°C (gas
mark 3) for 30 minutes. Remove
the bayleaf, sprinkle with the
parsley and serve.

SOUSED BABACO HERRINGS

PREPARATION TIME: *45 minutes*   **COOKING TIME:** *20 minutes*   **[M]**

Ingredients *(per 2 persons)*:

2 × 200 g (8 oz) herring (or
  mackerel)
Salt
100 g (4 oz) **Guernsey babaco**
50 g (2 oz) onion
100 ml (4 fl oz) water
25 ml (1 fl oz) white wine
  vinegar
15 g (½ oz) pickling spice
25 g (1 oz) cucumber, sliced

Method:

1 Gut and clean the herrings,
remove the fillets and wash well.
Pat dry with kitchen paper and
sprinkle with salt. Allow to
stand for 30 minutes.
2 Liquidise the babaco and
strain through a fine sieve.
3 Slice the onion and place in
the bottom of an ovenproof
dish. Roll each fillet around a
piece of onion and secure with a
cocktail stick. Place on top of
the onions.
4 Place the babaco purée,
water, vinegar and pickling spice
in a saucepan, bring to the boil
and simmer for 3 minutes. Pour
over the herring fillets.
5 Cover the fillets and bake in
an oven at 170°C (gas mark 3)
for 20 minutes.
6 Remove from the oven,
allow to cool in the cooking
liquid.
7 Remove and serve with slices
of cucumber.

Note: May be served hot or
cold.

LOBSTER WITH BABACO CREAM SAUCE

PREPARATION TIME: *30 minutes*   **COOKING TIME:** *15 minutes*   **[M]**

Ingredients *(per 2 persons)*:

100 g (4 oz) **Guernsey babaco**
1 × 600 g (1½ lb) lobster

25 g (1 oz) seasoned flour
25 g (1 oz) butter

25 g (1 oz) shallots, finely
  chopped
15 ml (½ oz) tomato purée
25 ml (1 fl oz) Cognac brandy
50 ml (2 fl oz) double cream
1 egg yolk
25 g (1 oz) white breadcrumbs

Method:

1 Liquidise the babaco and
pass through a fine sieve.
2 Split the lobster in half,
remove the gut and intestine.
Cut the tail meat into pieces and
crack the claws with a hammer
to remove the meat. Dip in the
seasoned flour. Wash and save
the 2 lobster halves.
3 Heat the butter in a pan and
sauté the lobster pieces. Remove
the lobster pieces and keep

warm. Add the shallots and fry
for 1 minute.
4 Add the tomato purée and
cook for a further minute.
5 Add the brandy and flame,
then add the babaco, bring to
the boil and reduce by half.
6 Return the lobster pieces to
the sauce, add the cream and
egg yolk (mixed together),
reheat (but do not boil) and
place into the 2 lobster shells.
7 Sprinkle with the
breadcrumbs and place under
the top grill until brown. Serve
immediately.

Note: If there is any coral (eggs)
these should be pounded with a
little butter, sieved and added to
the sauce with the egg yolk and
cream.

BAKED MACKEREL WITH BABACO SAUCE

PREPARATION TIME: *15 minutes*   **COOKING TIME:** *25 minutes*   **[M]**

Ingredients *(per person):*

1 × 150 g (6 oz) mackerel
25 g (1 oz) shallot
50 g (2 oz) butter
1 tablespoon white breadcrumbs
6 fresh sage leaves

½ teaspoon English mustard
  powder
100 g (4 oz) **Guernsey babaco**
½ teaspoon parsley, chopped

Method:

1   Remove the head from the fish, clean, wash and pat dry with kitchen paper.
2   Fry the shallots in half the butter until soft, add the breadcrumbs. Stuff the gut cavity and retain with wooden cocktail sticks.
3   Melt the remaining butter and lightly fry the sage (which has been finely shredded). Add the mustard.
4   Place the fish in a buttered dish, brush with the sage butter and bake in an oven at 200°C (gas mark 6) for 15–20 minutes.
5   Peel the babaco slice and liquidise the flesh. Place in a pan, bring to the boil and add the chopped parsley.
6   To serve: place the mackerel on a hot plate, remove the cocktail sticks and serve the babaco sauce separately.

Note: Other oily fish (herring, trout, salmon) may be used in place of the mackerel.

FRICASSÉE OF MONKFISH WITH BABACO AND GINGER

PREPARATION TIME: *20 minutes*   **COOKING TIME:** *15 minutes*   **[M]**

Ingredients *(per 2 persons)*:

300 g (12 oz) monkfish
50 g (2 oz) plain flour
Salt and milled white pepper
1 pinch cayenne pepper
25 g (1 oz) carrot
25 g (1 oz) courgette
25 g (1 oz) turnip
25 g (1 oz) butter
15 ml (½ fl oz) olive oil
200 g (8 oz) **Guernsey babaco**
15 g (½ oz) root ginger, grated
100 ml (4 fl oz) double cream

Method:

1   Cut the monkfish into goujons (strips) 8 × 2 cm (3 × ¾ in) and mix with the flour seasoned with salt, pepper and a little cayenne pepper.
2   Cut the vegetables into fine strips 5 × 0.5 cm (2 × ¼ in). Cook in a little boiling salted water for 5 minutes.
3   Heat the oil and butter and fry the monkfish until golden brown. Remove and keep warm.

4 Add the babaco which has been cut into strips 8 × 2 cm (3 × ¾ in) and ginger, fry for a minute.
5 Add the cream, bring to the boil. Return the monkfish to the

pan and reheat.
6 To serve: place the cooked vegetables as a border around the edge of the plate with the monkfish in the centre. Decorate with a fan of sliced babaco.

Recipe supplied by Ashley A. Huntley

MUSSELS ISLAND STYLE

PREPARATION TIME: *20 minutes*   **COOKING TIME:** *10 minutes*   **[M]**

Ingredients *(per 2 persons)*:

400 ml (1 pt) mussels
200 g (8 oz) **Guernsey babaco**
1 small kiwi fruit
25 ml (1 fl oz) olive oil
25 g shallots, diced
2 cloves garlic, diced
25 ml (1 fl oz) Muscadet (or other dry white wine).
¼ teaspoon oregano
2 tomatoes, skinned and depipped
Salt and milled black pepper

Method:

1 Scrub clean, de-beard and wash the mussels (discarding any that are open).
2 Cut the babaco into pieces and liquidise. Peel and dice the kiwi fruit.
3 Heat the oil in a thick-

bottomed pan, add the shallots and garlic and fry for 30 seconds.
4 Place the mussels in the pan, seal with a tight fitting lid and cook over a high flame for 3–4 minutes until all the mussels are open.
5 Add the white wine, babaco pulp, oregano, kiwi fruit and tomatoes, return to the heat and cook for a further 3–4 minutes. Check seasoning.
6 Serve in bowls with garlic bread [slices of bread buttered with garlic butter (minced garlic clove mixed in with the butter) and heated in a hot oven], finger bowls (a bowl of warm water and slice of lemon to wash the fingers) and a debris plate for the empty mussel shells.

MUSSEL, MUSHROOM AND BABACO PIE

PREPARATION TIME: *30 minutes* **COOKING TIME:** *45 minutes* **[M]**

Ingredients *(per 4 persons)*:

25 g (1 oz) shallots, finely diced
1 clove garlic, finely diced
25 g (1 oz) butter
25 g (1 oz) plain flour
250 ml (½ pt) full cream milk
100 g (4 oz) button mushrooms
200 g (8 oz) mussels (cooked, shelled)
200 g (8 oz) **Guernsey babaco**
50 g (2 oz) smoked bacon
Salt and milled black pepper
1 teaspoon parsley, chopped
150 g (6 oz) puff pastry
1 (size 3) egg

Method:

1 Fry the shallots and garlic in the butter until soft.
2 Add the flour, cook for 1 minute, then add the hot milk a little at a time, stirring continuously. Cook over a low heat for 10 minutes.
3 Add the mushrooms, mussels, babaco [cut into 1.5 cm (½ in) cubes] and the bacon cut into short, thin strips. Correct the seasoning, add the parsley and allow to cool.
4 Place the filling in a suitable pie dish.
5 Roll out the pastry to 0.5 cm (¼ in) thickness and cover the filling.
6 Make a small hole in the centre of the pastry, brush with beaten egg and bake in a hot oven at 200°C (gas mark 6) for 30 minutes until well risen and golden brown.
7 Serve immediately.

CURRIED BABACO AND PRAWNS

PREPARATION TIME: *15 minutes*   **COOKING TIME:** *45 minutes*   **[M]**

Ingredients: *(per 2 persons)*:

150 g (6 oz) **Guernsey babaco**
25 ml (1 fl oz) oil
25 g (1 oz) butter
1 large onion, diced
1 clove garlic
15 g (½ oz) curry powder
25 g (1 oz) tomato purée
250 ml (½ pt) fish stock
100 g (4 oz) prawns
2 tomatoes, skinned and
  depipped
15 g (½ oz) cornflour

Method:

1   Peel the babaco and cut into cubes. Squeeze the skin and save the juice.
2   Place the oil in a pan over a medium heat. Add the butter, diced onion and finely chopped garlic, and fry till soft.
3   Add the curry powder and cook for 1 minute, add the tomato purée and cook for a further minute.
4   Add the stock and babaco juice, bring to the boil and simmer for 30 minutes.
5   Add the babaco, prawns and tomatoes, bring back to the boil and thicken with the cornflour (slaked with a little cold water).
6   Serve with poached patna rice, poppadums and a selection of condiments (toasted coconut, diced onion, lime pickle, sultanas, etc.).

SALMON STEAK SAINT PIERRE

PREPARATION TIME: *20 minutes*   **COOKING TIME:** *15 minutes*   **[M]**

Ingredients *(per 2 persons)*:

100 g (4 oz) **Guernsey babaco**
50 g (2 oz) butter

½ teaspoon anchovy essence
2 hard-boiled egg yolks

1 teaspoon tarragon, shredded
Salt and milled white pepper
2 × 150 g (6 oz) salmon steaks

Method:

1 Cut the babaco in half then
into 1 cm (⅓ in) slices.
2 Cream 25 g (1 oz) of the
butter with the anchovy essence
and the sieved hard-boiled egg
yolks. Add the shredded

tarragon. Keep the butter soft
but not melted.
3 Season the steaks, brush with
the remaining butter (melted)
and bake in an oven at 200°C
(gas mark 6) for 5 minutes.
4 Remove, top with the babaco
slices and spread the babaco
with the butter. Return to the
oven and bake for a further 10
minutes. Serve immediately.

SUPRÊME OF SALMON WITH DILL BABACO

PREPARATION TIME: *15 minutes*   **COOKING TIME:** *15 minutes*   **[M]**

Ingredients *(per person)*:

100 g (4 oz) **Guernsey babaco**
2 tablespoons fresh dill
25 g (1 oz) seasoned flour
25 g (1 oz) butter
150 g (6 oz) salmon fillet
25 ml (1 fl oz) oil

Method:

1 Cut the babaco in half and
then into 1 cm (⅓ in) slices.
Allow to drain to remove excess
juices.
2 Chop the dill and mix one-
third into the seasoned flour.
3 Blend the remaining dill with
half the butter together with the

babaco juice. Chill in a
refrigerator.
4 Cut the fillet in two
lengthways and remove the skin
and any bones. Coat the fillets
with the seasoned flour, pressing
it well into the two pieces.
5 Fry the salmon pieces in the
oil for 2 minutes each side,
remove and keep hot.
6 Drain the frying pan of the
oil, add the remaining butter
and lightly fry the babaco slices.
7 Place the salmon fillet on a
hot plate, dress the babaco slices
neatly on top and finally add the
dill butter. Serve immediately.

COQUILLES SAINT JACQUES TORTEVAL

PREPARATION TIME: *10 minutes* **COOKING TIME:** *5 minutes*

Ingredients *(per person)*:

50 g (2 oz) **Guernsey babaco**
2–3 scallops
25 g (1 oz) seasoned flour
1 tablespoon oil
15 g (½ oz) butter
1 clove garlic
25 ml (1 fl oz) **babaco** juice
25 ml (1 fl oz) Cognac brandy
15 ml (½ fl oz) Guernsey cream
1 dessertspoon chives, chopped

Method:

1 Peel the babaco and cut the flesh into cubes. The skin can be squeezed to produce some of the babaco juice required.
2 Dip the scallops into the seasoned flour (slice if large).
3 Place the oil into a flambé pan (or frying pan) and add the butter. Quickly fry the finely chopped garlic. Add the scallops and brown all over.
4 Add the babaco pieces and babaco juice and bring to the boil. Simmer until reduced by half, basting the scallops.
5 Add the Cognac brandy and flame, douse with the cream and finish with the chopped chives.

SCAMPIS MOULIN HUET

PREPARATION TIME: *15 minutes* **COOKING TIME:** *30 minutes* **[M]**

Ingredients *(per 2 persons)*:

1 × 400 g (1 lb) **Guernsey babaco**
1 teaspoon breadcrumbs
1 teaspoon parmesan cheese
1 teaspoon parsley, chopped
200 g (8 oz) peeled scampi
25 g (1 oz) seasoned flour
50 g (2 oz) smoked ham
25 g (1 oz) shallots, diced
25 g (1 oz) butter
25 ml (1 fl oz) Cognac brandy

Method:

1 The babaco should be half of a whole fruit cut lengthways (boat-shaped). Scoop out the soft centre.

2 Mix the breadcrumbs, cheese and parsley together.

3 Dip the scampi in the seasoned flour.

4 Fry the ham and shallots in the butter, add the scampi and cook for 2 minutes.

5 Add the brandy and flame.

Place in the babaco half, sprinkle with the breadcrumb mixture.

6 Bake in an oven at 200°C (gas mark 6) for 15–20 minutes.

7 Serve with rice that has been simmered in fish stock.

Note: If a microwave oven with no browning facility is used the dish should be browned under a top grill.

STUFFED SEA BREAM WITH BABACO AND ALMONDS

PREPARATION TIME: *30 minutes*   **COOKING TIME:** *30 minutes*   **[M]**

Ingredients *(per 2 persons)*:

100 g (4 oz) **Guernsey babaco**
25 g (1 oz) breadcrumbs
1 × 800 g (2 lb) sea bream
25 g (1 oz) butter
25 g (1 oz) shallots, finely
  chopped
1 clove garlic, finely diced
25 g (1 oz) almonds, flaked
1 piece fresh ginger
1 hard boiled egg

Method:

1 Cut the babaco into pieces and liquidise. Add the breadcrumbs and allow to stand

for 10 minutes.

2 Remove the gills from the bream and draw out the gut from the gill cavity. Scrape away the scales and wash the fish well.

3 Melt the butter in a pan and fry the shallots and garlic. Add the almonds and shredded ginger and fry for 1 minute. Add the babaco mixture and simmer for 5 minutes until thickened.

4 Stuff the gut cavity with the babaco stuffing and either sew or seal with cocktail sticks.

5 Score the back of the fish, brush with melted butter and

either bake in an oven at 200°C
(gas mark 6) for 20 minutes
(basting regularly), or grill

(10 minutes each side).
6 Serve with sieved hard boiled
egg.

FRIED SKATE WITH BABACO AND SAGE SAUCE

PREPARATION TIME: *30 minutes*   **COOKING TIME:** *25 minutes*   **[M]**

Ingredients *(per 2 persons)*:

150 g (6 oz) **Guernsey babaco**
400 g (1 lb) skate wing
1 litre (2 pt) water
1 level teaspoon salt
25 ml (1 fl oz) malt vinegar
50 g (2 oz) butter
2 egg yolks
Salt and milled black pepper
1 teaspoon fresh sage
50 g (2 oz) seasoned flour

Method:

1 Peel the babaco and liquidise
the flesh. Squeeze the skin and
save the juice. Heat almost to
the boil.
2 Wash and scrub the skate
wing in salted water, place in a
pan with water, salt and vinegar.
Bring to the boil and simmer for
2 minutes. Remove and allow to
cool.

3 Melt 25 g (1 oz) of the butter
and whisk into the egg yolks
over a pan of boiling water until
thick and creamy. Slowly whisk
in the babaco pulp, season with
salt and pepper, add the fresh
sage (cut into fine strips) and
keep warm.
4 Scrape away the skin from
the skate and cut into suitable
portions. Dip in the seasoned
flour and fry in the remaining
butter.
5 Place the skate pieces onto a
suitable dish and coat with the
babaco sauce. Serve
immediately.

Note: If the sauce splits, whisk
into another raw egg yolk a little
at a time.

FILETS DE SOLE CARICA

PREPARATION TIME: *15 minutes*   **COOKING TIME:** *15 minutes*   **[M]**

Ingredients *(per 2 persons)*:

200 g (8 oz) **Guernsey babaco**
75 g (3 oz) white breadcrumbs
1 teaspoon parsley, chopped
25 g (1 oz) smoked ham
75 g (3 oz) butter
2 × 100–150 g (4–6 oz) sole
    fillets
25 g (1 oz) seasoned flour

Method:

1 Peel the babaco, cut the flesh
into 1 cm (⅓ in) cubes. Squeeze
the skin and save the juice.
2 Mix together the
breadcrumbs, finely chopped
parsley and smoked (diced)
ham.

3 Melt half the butter, dip the
fillets into the seasoned flour,
then into the butter and finally
into the breadcrumbs. Lay on a
buttered tray.
4 Stew the diced babaco in a
small knob of the butter and any
of the babaco juices for
approximately 5 minutes.
5 Melt the remaining butter
and pour over the fillets. Grill
the fillets for 4–5 minutes under
a salamander (top grill) or bake
in a hot oven 200°C (gas
mark 6) for 5–6 minutes.
6 Place the fillets on a serving
dish and serve the stewed
babaco around the fillets.

TURBOT AND BABACO MOUSSE WITH ORANGE SAUCE

PREPARATION TIME: *1 hour*   **COOKING TIME:** *20 minutes*

Ingredients *(per 4 persons)*:

Turbot mousse:
200 g (8 oz) turbot fillet
1 egg white

125 ml (5 fl oz) double cream
Salt and milled white pepper

Babaco mousse:
200 g (8 oz) **Guernsey babaco**
125 ml (5 fl oz) double cream
1 egg white
Salt and milled white pepper
Orange sauce:
25 ml (1 fl oz) Cointreau
50 ml (2 fl oz) fresh orange juice
250 ml (½ pt) double cream
4 sprigs of fresh dill

Method:

1 Skin the turbot, mince the fillet twice and pass through a sieve. Place in a bowl over ice and gradually beat in the egg white until the mixture becomes stiff.
2 Whip the cream until thick (but not peaked) and fold into the turbot mixture. Season with salt and pepper and store in the refrigerator.
3 *To make the babaco mousse:* Peel and chop the babaco and liquidise. Pass the purée through a fine sieve. Whip the cream

until thick (but not peaked). Whisk the egg white until peaked and fold into the purée together with the cream. Season and store in the refrigerator.
4 Butter 4 stainless-steel coupe dishes and half-fill with the turbot mousse leaving a hole in the centre. Fill the hole with the babaco mousse.
5 Cover each with buttered kitchen foil and cook in a pan of boiling water in an oven at 150°C (gas mark 2) for 15 minutes.
6 Meanwhile heat a small saucepan, add the liqueur, and flame. Add the orange juice and reduce by half. Add the cream, bring to the boil and reduce until thickened.
7 To serve: remove the dishes from the water and stand for 2–3 minutes. Flood the warmed fish plates with the orange sauce and turn out the mousses onto the centre. Garnish with a sprig of fresh dill. Serve immediately.

Recipe supplied by Geoffrey E. Austin

Meat

BABACO MEAT MARINADE

PREPARATION TIME: *15 minutes*

Ingredients *(per 4 persons)*:

100 g (4 oz) carrots
100 g (4 oz) onions
100 g (4 oz) celery
100 g (4 oz) leeks
200 g (8 oz) **Guernsey babaco**
500 ml (1 pt) water
12 peppercorns
1 bayleaf
2 parsley stalks

Method:

1 Peel and cut the vegetables into 2 cm (¾ in) pieces (*mirepoix*).

2 Liquidise the babaco, add to the vegetables, water and herbs.
3 Prepare the meat (either as a whole joint or cut into pieces). Place into the marinade, making sure the meat is completely submerged.
4 The length of time needed for the meat to stay in the marinade depends on the joint used (the tougher the longer). 12 hours should be sufficient in most cases.
5 Use the marinade as part of the cooking stock.

BABACO FERMIÈRE

PREPARATION TIME: *20 minutes* COOKING TIME: *1¼ hours* **[M]**

Ingredients *(per 2 persons)*:

300 g (12 oz) topside of beef
50 g (2 oz) seasoned flour

25 g (1 oz) butter
100 g (4 oz) onions

38

15 g (½ oz) tomato purée
100 ml (4 fl oz) brown stock
25 g (1 oz) soft brown sugar
50 ml (2 fl oz) **babaco** juice
150 g (6 oz) **Guernsey babaco**
250 ml (½ pt) brown ale
1 teaspoon parsley, chopped

Method:

1 Thinly slice the beef, beat
the slices thoroughly. Dip in the
seasoned flour.
2 Lightly fry the beef in the
butter, remove and fry the sliced
onions until brown. Return the

beef to the pan, add the tomato
purée, sugar, stock, babaco juice
and brown ale. Bring to the
boil, cover and place in an oven
at 180°C (gas mark 4) for 30
minutes.
3 Cut the babaco in half then
into 1 cm (½ in) slices. Add to
the beef, return to the oven and
cook for a further 30 minutes.
4 *To serve:* remove from the
oven, strain and place the beef,
babaco and onions in a serving
dish. Reduce the cooking liquid,
pour over the beef, dress with
chopped parsley and serve.

BEEFY BABACO BOATS

PREPARATION TIME: *20 minutes* **COOKING TIME:** *1¼ hours*   **[M]**

Ingredients *(per 2 persons)*:

1 medium sized **Guernsey
  babaco**
50 g (2 oz) onion, diced
25 g (1 oz) butter
1 clove garlic
Salt and milled black pepper
200 g (8 oz) lean minced beef
25 g (1 oz) plain flour
15 g (½ oz) tomato purée
100 ml (4 fl oz) brown stock
½ teaspoon oregano
25 g (1 oz) parmesan cheese
15 g (½ oz) white breadcrumbs
½ teaspoon parsley, chopped

Method:

1 Cut the babaco in half
lengthways and scoop out the
soft feathery centre.
2 Fry the onion and finely
chopped garlic in the butter, add
the seasoned beef, cook for 2
minutes, add the flour and cook
for a further 2 minutes. Add the
tomato purée, cook for 1 minute
and gradually stir in the boiling
stock. Add the oregano and
simmer for 30 minutes, stirring
regularly.
3 Place the babaco halves in a
lightly buttered, heat-proof dish

and fill the centre with the beef mixture.

4 Mix the parmesan cheese, breadcrumbs and chopped parsley together and heap on top of the beef.

5 Bake in a hot oven at 200°C (gas mark 6) for 15 minutes until the topping is brown. Serve.

Note: Other meats such as lamb, pork, veal, chicken can be used in place of the beef and other herbs, such as thyme, majoram and sage can be used in place of the oregano.

GUERNSEY BURGER

PREPARATION TIME: *10 minutes* **COOKING TIME:** *10 minutes*

Ingredients *(per person)*:

1 × 100–160 g (4–6 oz) beefburger
50 g (2 oz) slice **Guernsey babaco**
1 teaspoon thyme, chopped
1 teaspoon white breadcrumbs
50 g (2 oz) Guernsey cheese (or Cheddar cheese)

Method:

1 Grill the beefburger for 2–3 minutes on each side.

2 The babaco should be in a 1 cm (⅓ in) slice.

3 Place the babaco slice on top of the beefburger, mix the thyme with the breadcrumbs and place in the centre of the babaco.

4 Place the cheese (in a slice) on top of the babaco and then grill until the cheese is bubbling and brown. Serve immediately.

MEAT BALLS IN SPICY BABACO SAUCE

PREPARATION TIME: *45 minutes* **COOKING TIME:** *45 minutes* **[M]**

Ingredients *(per 2 persons)*:

2 slices white bread
200 g (8 oz) minced lean beef

25 g (1 oz) onions, finely diced
1 clove garlic, finely diced

1 teaspoon parsley, finely
  chopped
Salt and milled black pepper
1 (size 2) egg
Sauce:
1 × 396 g (14 oz) can plum
  tomatoes
100 g (4 oz) **Guernsey babaco**
25 ml (1 fl oz) olive oil
50 g (2 oz) onions, diced
1 clove garlic
15 g (½ oz) plain flour
2 teaspoons Tabasco sauce
½ teaspoon chervil, chopped

Method:

1 Remove the crusts from the
bread and soak in a little water.
Squeeze out excess water.

2 Mix the beef, bread, onion,
garlic, parsley, black pepper and
egg. Bind together and form
into balls the size of a cherry.
3 *To make the sauce:* liquidise
the tomatoes and babaco and
pass through a sieve.
4 Heat the oil in a pan, fry the
onion and minced garlic, add the
flour, cook for 1 minute. Add
the babaco and tomato mixture
and bring to the boil. Add the
Tabasco sauce.
5 Quickly fry the meat balls in
hot fat to seal and brown, add
to the sauce and simmer for 30
minutes over a low flame.
6 Finish with chopped chervil
and serve with pasta or mashed
potatoes.

ROAST BEEF CAREY

PREPARATION TIME: *20 minutes* **COOKING TIME:** *1½ hours*   **[M]**

Ingredients *(per 4 persons)*:

800 g (2 lb) topside of beef
Salt and milled black pepper
2 cloves garlic
25 g (1 oz) lard
300 g (12 oz) **Guernsey babaco**
50 g (2 oz) horseradish sauce

Method:

1 Season the beef well with salt
and pepper.

2 Make some small incisions in
the joint and place slivers of
garlic in them. Tie or skewer the
joint if necessary.
3 Place the joint into a roasting
tin, baste with the melted lard
and seal in a hot oven at 200°C
(gas mark 6) for 20 minutes.
4 Turn temperature down to
150°C (gas mark 2) and roast for
a further hour.

5 *Whilst the joint is roasting:*
Cut four 1 cm (⅓ in) slices from
the babaco, liquidise the
remaining babaco and mix it
with the horseradish.
6 For the last 20 minutes
cooking of the joint, place the
babaco slices on top and fill the
centres with the babaco and
horseradish mixture.
7 Serve in thin slices with the
cooked babaco rings, gravy
(made by de-glazing the roasting
pan with a little beef stock) and
any remaining babaco and
horseradish mixture.

Recipe supplied by Edith Carey

SPICY BABACO BEEF

PREPARATION TIME: *15 minutes* **COOKING TIME:** *35 minutes* **[M]**

Ingredients *(per person)*:

150 g (6 oz) minced lean beef
Salt and milled black pepper
1 teaspoon chilli powder
50 g (2 oz) onion, diced
1 clove garlic, diced
15 g (½ oz) butter
15 g (½ oz) plain flour
25 g (1 oz) tomato purée
175 ml (⅓ pt) beef stock
50 g (2 oz) red kidney beans
100 g (4 oz) **Guernsey babaco**
1 tomato, skinned and depipped
½ teaspoon parsley, chopped

Method:

1 Season the beef with salt and
pepper and the chilli powder.
2 Fry the onion and garlic in
the butter, add the beef and
cook for 2–3 minutes. Add the
flour and cook for 1 minute,
then add the tomato purée.
Blend in the hot stock a little at
a time stirring well, bringing it
back to the boil after each
addition.
3 Add the kidney beans and
simmer over a low heat for 20
minutes.
4 Peel and dice the babaco,
add to the beef (including any
juices) and simmer for a further
10 minutes. Add the diced
tomato, finely chopped parsley
and serve.
5 Serve with poached patna
rice (cooked in white meat
stock).

BABACO AND LAMB RISSOLES

PREPARATION TIME: *30 minutes* **COOKING TIME:** *30 minutes*

Ingredients *(per 2 persons)*:

100 g (4 oz) **Guernsey babaco**
25 g (1 oz) shallots, finely diced
1 clove garlic, finely diced
25 g (1 oz) butter
100 g (4 oz) minced lean lamb
15 g (½ oz) plain flour
10 g (⅓ oz) tomato purée
50 ml (2 fl oz) white stock
½ teaspoon oregano, chopped
Salt and milled black pepper
200 g (8 oz) puff pastry
1 egg yolk

Method:

1 Liquidise the babaco.
2 Fry the shallots and garlic in the butter, add the seasoned minced lamb and cook for 2–3 minutes.
3 Add the flour and cook for 1 minute, then add the tomato purée and cook for a further minute.
4 Gradually add the stock and babaco purée stirring constantly, bring to the boil and simmer until sauce has thickened (10–15 minutes).
5 Add the oregano, check seasoning and allow to cool.
6 Roll out the puff pastry to 2 mm (¹⁄₁₀ in) thick. Cut into 13 cm (5 in) diameter rounds.
7 Moisten the edges of the circles with egg yolk and place a dessertspoon of lamb mixture in the centre of each. Fold in half to form a semi-circle and seal the edges well.
8 Heat the oil to 175°C and deep fry the rissoles until well puffed and brown. Drain on kitchen paper and serve.

LAMB CUTLETS HEILBORN

PREPARATION TIME: *30 minutes* **COOKING TIME:** *30 minutes*   [M]

Ingredients *(per 2 persons)*:

600 g (1½ lb) best end of lamb
  (6 bones)

50 g (2 oz) seasoned flour
200 g (8 oz) **Guernsey babaco**

25 g (1 oz) butter
15 ml (½ fl oz) light soy sauce
1 clove garlic, finely chopped
1 teaspoon root ginger, finely
   chopped
25 g (1 oz) clear honey
Oil for frying.
½ teaspoon parsley, finely
   chopped

Method:

1   Chine (remove backbone)
and trim the best end of skin
and excess fat. Scrape the bones
clean approximately 2.5 cm
(1 in) along the end. Cut each
cutlet between the bones and
lightly batten out. Dip in the
seasoned flour.

2   Liquidise the babaco, melt
the butter, add the babaco pulp,
soy sauce, garlic, ginger and
honey and bring to the boil.
Simmer for 5 minutes.

3   Fry the cutlets in the hot oil
to seal and brown, then place in
an ovenproof dish. Coat with
the babaco mixture and cook for
15–20 minutes in a hot oven at
200°C (gas mark 6).

4   Remove from the oven,
place the cutlets on a serving
dish and keep warm. Reduce
cooking liquid, correct the
seasoning and coat the cutlets.
Sprinkle with the chopped
parsley and serve.

SADDLE OF LAMB WITH GLAZED BABACO

PREPARATION TIME: *20 minutes* **COOKING TIME:** *2 hours*

Ingredients *(per 6–8 persons)*:

1 medium dressed saddle of
   lamb
Salt and milled black pepper
50 g (2 oz) butter
4 cloves garlic
6 sprigs rosemary
50 g (2 oz) clear honey
600 g (1½ lb) **Guernsey babaco**
250 ml (½ pt) brown lamb stock
10 g (⅓ oz) cornflour

Method:

1   Rub the saddle with salt and
pepper and place on a roasting
tray.
2   Melt the butter in a
saucepan, add the crushed
garlic, cloves, rosemary and
honey, bring to the boil and
pour over the saddle.
3   Place the saddle in an oven
at 170°C (gas mark 3) and roast

for 20 minutes for each 400 g
(1 lb) of joint weight. Baste
every 15 minutes.
4 Meanwhile cut the babaco in
half and then into 1.5 cm (½ in)
slices.
5 On completion of cooking,
remove the joint from the oven
and lay the babaco slices neatly
along the centre of the saddle.
Baste the babaco well with the
juices and return to the oven for

a further 30 minutes, basting
every 10 minutes.
6 Remove from the oven, put
the saddle on a warm plate and
keep hot. Add the stock to the
meat juices, strain into a
saucepan, remove excess fat,
add the cornflour slaked with a
little cold water, correct the
seasoning. Serve the gravy with
the lamb carved in thick slices
and the slices of babaco.

EASTERN PORK

PREPARATION TIME: *45 minutes*   **COOKING TIME:** *20 minutes*   **[M]**

Ingredients *(per person)*:

150 g (6 oz) pork fillet
Salt and milled black pepper
25 ml (1 fl oz) oil (or butter)
1 clove garlic
100 g (4 oz) **Guernsey babaco**
25 g (1 oz) onions, diced
50 ml (2 fl oz) white meat stock
25 ml (1 fl oz) Muscadet (or
  other dry white wine)
15 g (½ oz) cornflour
25 g (1 oz) button mushrooms
1 tomato, skinned and depipped
15 g (½ oz) spring onion (green)
  or chives
1 teaspoon parsley, chopped

Method:

1 Cut the pork into cubes,
season with salt and pepper and

place in a bowl with oil and
finely chopped garlic. Allow to
stand for 30 minutes.
2 Peel the babaco over a bowl
to collect the juices and cut into
cubes (squeeze the skin and
collect the juice).
3 Heat a deep pan until very
hot. Add pork cubes and fry
until brown and sealed. Add
diced onions and fry for 2
minutes.
4 Add the stock, wine and
babaco juice, bring to the boil
and simmer for 10 minutes.
5 Slake the cornflour with a
little cold water and then add to
the pork and bring to the boil
stirring constantly. Add the
mushrooms (sliced), tomato,

babaco and spring onions and simmer for 2 minutes until heated through.

6 Sprinkle with chopped parsley and serve with boiled patna rice or buttered noodles.

ROAST BABACO-STUFFED BELLY PORK

PREPARATION TIME: *30 minutes* **COOKING TIME:** *2 hours*

Ingredients *(per 4 persons)*:

800 g (2 lb) belly of pork joint
Salt and milled white pepper
300 g (12 oz) **Guernsey babaco**
Oil for cooking
25 ml (1 fl oz) brandy
100 ml (4 fl oz) white meat stock
15 g (½ oz) castor sugar
50 ml (2 fl oz) water
15 g (½ oz) arrowroot

Method:

1 Score the skin of the joint and remove any bones. Rub well with salt and pepper on both sides.
2 Slice one-third of the babaco and lay the slices along the flesh side of the joint. Roll joint and tie with string (or use skewers). Place in a roasting dish, coat with a little oil.
3 Place in a hot oven 200°C (gas mark 6) for 30 minutes then reduce to 180°C (gas mark 4) for 1½ hours.
4 When cooked, remove the joint and keep warm. Drain excess fat, place roasting dish over flame, add brandy and set alight. Add the stock to deglaze the pan. Bring the gravy to the boil, check seasoning.
5 Peel and liquidise the remaining babaco, add sugar and water, bring to the boil and thicken with the arrowroot (slaked with a little cold water).
6 To serve: remove the string (or skewers), cut into thick slices and serve with the gravy and hot babaco sauce.

Recipe supplied by Christine Goodlass

SWEET-N-SOUR PORK WITH BABACO

PREPARATION TIME: *40 minutes* **COOKING TIME:** *20 minutes*

Ingredients *(per 2 persons)*:

Pork:
300 g (12 oz) lean pork
Salt
15 ml (½ fl oz) soy sauce
1 (size 5) egg
15 g (½ oz) cornflour
Sauce:
200 g (8 oz) **Guernsey babaco**
50 ml (2 fl oz) **babaco** juice
15 ml (½ fl oz) dry sherry
15 ml (½ fl oz) white wine
    vinegar
15 g (½ oz) tomato purée
25 g (1 oz) granulated sugar
½ teaspoon ground ginger
15 g (½ oz) cornflour
3 spring onions, chopped

Method:

1 Dice the pork into 1.5 cm (¾ in) pieces and place in a bowl with the salt and soy sauce, stand for 1 hour.
2 Mix the egg with the cornflour, pre-heat the oil to 175°C, dip the pork pieces into the egg batter and deep fry in the hot oil until golden brown. Drain on absorbent kitchen paper and keep warm.
3 *For the sauce:* cut the babaco into 1.5 cm (¾ in) slices, peel and cut into cubes. Squeeze the skin and save the juice.
4 Place the babaco juice, sherry, vinegar, tomato purée, sugar and ginger in a saucepan, bring to the boil and thicken with the cornflour which has firstly been slaked with a little cold water. Add the babaco cubes and cook for 5 minutes. If too thick add a little water.
5 *To serve:* place the cooked pork into the sauce, top with the finely chopped spring onions and serve with plain boiled long grain rice.

SWEET BRAISED PORK

PREPARATION TIME: *15 minutes* **COOKING TIME:** *1½ hours* **[M]**

Ingredients *(per person)*:

1 × 150–200 g (6–8 oz) pork chop
25 g (1 oz) seasoned flour
50 g (2 oz) onion, sliced
2 tomatoes, skinned and sliced
100 g (4 oz) **Guernsey babaco**
2 potatoes, peeled
125 ml (¼ pt) white meat stock
25 g (1 oz) butter
½ teaspoon parsley, chopped

Method:

1 Trim most of the fat from the chop, dip in the seasoned flour, seal and brown in hot fat.
2 Place the chop in an ovenproof dish on half of the sliced onions. Place the remaining onions and tomatoes on top.
3 Cut the babaco in half, slice thinly and lay on top of the onions and tomatoes.
4 Slice the potatoes and layer (overlapping) so that the babaco is completely covered.
5 Pour over the stock and brush the potato slices with melted butter.
6 Cook in an oven at 150°C (gas mark 2) for 1½ hours, pressing the potatoes under the stock to prevent them drying out. The potatoes should be brown when the dish is cooked.
7 Sprinkle with chopped parsley and serve.

BACON AND BABACO CASSEROLE

PREPARATION TIME: *30 minutes* **COOKING TIME:** *45 minutes* **[M]**

Ingredients *(per 2 persons)*:

300 g (12 oz) smoked back
   bacon (uncut)
15 g (½ oz) butter

50 g (2 oz) seasoned flour
50 g (2 oz) onions, sliced
200 g (8 oz) **Guernsey babaco**

25 ml (1 fl oz) Calvados
125 ml (¼ pt) dry cider
¼ teaspoon fresh thyme,
   chopped
25 ml (1 fl oz) cream
Salt and milled black pepper
½ teaspoon parsley, chopped

Method:

1   Trim the bacon of all fat and
rind. Place the rind with the
butter and a little water in a
saucepan and stew for 15
minutes to extract some of the
fat.
2   Cut the bacon fillet into 4 ×
1 cm (⅓ in) slices, dip in the
seasoned flour.

3   Strain the butter and fat,
return to clean pan and fry the
fillets until brown. Remove and
place in an ovenproof dish.
4   Fry the onions and add to
the bacon.
5   Cut the babaco in half, then
into 1 cm (⅓ in) slices and add
to the bacon.
6   Add the Calvados and cider
to the butter together with the
thyme. Pour over the bacon,
cover and braise in an oven at
170°C (gas mark 3) for 45
minutes.
7   Remove from the oven, add
the cream, correct the
seasoning, dress with chopped
parsley and serve.

BRAISED HAM PRINCE ALBERT

PREPARATION TIME: *30 minutes* **COOKING TIME:** *1½ hours*   **[M]**

Ingredients *(per 4 persons)*:

300 g (12 oz) **Guernsey babaco**
600 g (1½ lb) smoked ham
1 bayleaf
12 peppercorns
2–3 parsley stalks
200 g (8 oz) carrot, onion, leek
   and celery
50 g (2 oz) onions, sliced
25 g (1 oz) butter
25 g (1 oz) plain flour
25 g (1 oz) tomato purée

25 ml (1 fl oz) dry Madeira
2 medium tomatoes
50 g (2 oz) black grapes
½ teaspoon fresh thyme,
   chopped

Method:

1   Put aside 4 thin half slices
from the babaco for garnish and
liquidise the remainder.
2   Place the ham in cold water

with a bayleaf, 12 peppercorns, parsley stalks and *mirepoix* (carrot, onion, celery and leek roughly chopped), bring to the boil and simmer for 1 hour. Allow to cool in the cooking liquid.

3 Fry the onion in the butter, add the flour and cook for 1 minute. Add the tomato purée and cook for a further minute.

4 Gradually add the babaco purée stirring constantly. Add approximately 250 ml (½ pt) of the cooking liquid and bring to the boil.

5 Slice the ham into medium thick slices and lay in an ovenproof dish. Sprinkle the ham with the Madeira and add the sauce.

6 Cover and braise in an oven at 170°C (gas mark 3) for 30 minutes.

7 Meanwhile, skin the tomatoes, depip and dice.

8 During the last 10 minutes of cooking add the tomatoes, babaco slices and grapes (halved and depipped).

9 Remove from the oven, correct seasoning, sprinkle with the chopped fresh thyme and serve.

BABACO TAGLIATELLE

PREPARATION TIME: *10 minutes* **COOKING TIME:** *20 minutes*

Ingredients *(per person)*:

50 g (2 oz) green tagliatelle
100 g (4 oz) **Guernsey babaco**
50 g (2 oz) prosciutto ham
2 cloves garlic
50 g (2 oz) butter
25 g (1 oz) parmesan cheese
Salt and milled black pepper

Method:

1 Cook the tagliatelle in plenty of boiling salted water for 10–12 minutes. Drain well.

2 Whilst the tagliatelle is cooking cut the babaco into small cubes after first peeling.

3 Cut the ham into strips. Fry the garlic in the butter, add the ham and cook for 2 minutes.

4 Add the babaco and any juices and cook for a further 2 minutes.

5 Fold in the tagliatelle and mix well with half the parmesan cheese.

6 Place in a serving dish and sprinkle with the remaining parmesan.

GRILLED GAMMON AND BABACO

PREPARATION TIME: *10 minutes*   **COOKING TIME:** 8 minutes   **[M]**

Ingredients *(per person)*:

25 g (1 oz) butter
½ teaspoon clear honey
15 g (½ oz) soft brown sugar
150 g (6 oz) gammon steak
1.5 cm (½ in) slice **Guernsey babaco**
¼ teaspoon parsley, chopped

Method:

1   Melt the butter, add the honey and soft brown sugar and dissolve.
2   Brush the steak with the mixture and grill over (or under) a brisk flame (3 minutes each side).
3   Place the babaco slice on top, brush with the butter mixture and grill for a further 2 minutes.
4   Sprinkle with chopped parsley and serve.

Note: The gammon may be cooked in a hot oven at 240°C (gas mark 9).

This dish may also be cooked in a microwave oven with a browning facility.

GUERNSEY VEAL OLIVES

PREPARATION TIME: *20 minutes*   **COOKING TIME:** *30 minutes*   **[M]**

Ingredients *(per 2 persons)*:

150 g (6 oz) **Guernsey babaco**
25 g (1 oz) shallots
50 g (2 oz) butter
50 g (2 oz) white breadcrumbs
Salt and milled white pepper
¼ teaspoon thyme, chopped
2 × 150 g (6 oz) veal escalopes

25 ml (1 fl oz) olive oil
2 cloves garlic
2 tomatoes, skinned and depipped
125 ml (¼ pt) white meat stock
1 teaspoon parsley, chopped

Method:

1 Peel the babaco and liquidise the flesh. Squeeze the skin and save the juice.

2 Fry the shallots in 25 g (1 oz) of the butter, add the breadcrumbs and enough babaco purée to produce a moist stuffing. Season with salt and pepper, add the thyme and cool.

3 Lightly beat the veal slices and spread the stuffing over them. Fold the left and right sides inwards and roll up to form a parcel. Tie with string or secure with cocktail sticks. Season with salt and pepper.

4 Heat the oil, add the remaining butter and fry the veal 'olives' to seal. Remove. Fry the garlic and tomato (diced), add the stock and any babaco purée left together with the babaco juice.

5 Place the olives in a heat-proof dish, add the liquid and cook in an oven at 180°C (gas mark 4) for 30 minutes (basting every 10 minutes).

6 Remove the string/cocktail sticks, decorate with the chopped parsley and serve.

VEAL ESCALOPE RONCEFER

PREPARATION TIME: *30 minutes* **COOKING TIME:** *10 minutes*

Ingredients *(per 2 persons)*:

25 g (1 oz) shallots, chopped
50 g (2 oz) butter
25 g (1 oz) Dijon mustard
200 g (8 oz) **Guernsey babaco**
100 g (4 oz) white breadcrumbs
2 × 150 g (6 oz) veal escalopes
1 teaspoon parsley, chopped
25 g (1 oz) ham, diced
50 g (2 oz) seasoned flour
1 (size 1) egg
2 sprigs fresh parsley

Method:

1 Lightly fry the shallots in 25 g (1 oz) of the butter. Add the mustard and 50 g (2 oz) of the babaco (chopped into a purée). Cook for 2 minutes, add a teaspoon of the breadcrumbs and allow to cool.

2 Beat the escalopes until wafer thin (but unbroken).

3 Place the mustard mixture into the centre of the escalopes and fold the escalopes to form a

seal around the stuffing. Pin
with a cocktail stick (making
sure the ends are protruding for
easy removal).

4 Mix the parsley and ham
with the breadcrumbs. Dip the
escalopes into the seasoned
flour, beaten egg and finally into
the breadcrumbs, making sure
they are well coated.

5 Cut the remaining babaco
into thin slices and gently stew
in the remaining butter.

6 Deep fry the escalopes in
medium hot oil (175°C) until
golden brown. Drain on kitchen
paper and remove the cocktail
stick.

7 Serve with the stewed babaco
and sprigs of deep fried parsley.

CALF'S LIVER GUERNSEY STYLE

PREPARATION TIME: *15 minutes* **COOKING TIME:** *15 minutes* **[M]**

Ingredients *(per person)*:

150 g (6 oz) calf's liver
½ teaspoon English mustard
 powder
25 g (1 oz) seasoned flour
1 tomato
50 g (2 oz) **Guernsey babaco**
50 g (2 oz) smoked bacon
50 g (2 oz) onions, sliced
25 ml (1 fl oz) oil
50 ml (2 fl oz) brown meat stock
25 ml (1 fl oz) medium-dry
 sherry
½ teaspoon parsley, chopped

Method:

1 Trim the liver, mix the dry
mustard powder with the
seasoned flour and dip the liver
in the flour mixture.

2 Skin, depip the tomato and
dice. Slice the babaco thinly.

3 Cut the bacon into strips
2.5 cm (1 in) long and fry
together with the onions.
Remove from the oil and keep
warm.

4 Fry the liver for 2 minutes on
each side.

5 Add the stock and sherry
and bring to the boil.

6 Mix in the bacon, onion,
tomato and babaco slices, cover
with a lid and simmer for
5 minutes.

7 Correct the seasoning,
decorate with the chopped
parsley and serve.

Note: Lamb's liver or pig's liver
may be used in place of the
calf's liver.

ROGNONS D'AGNEAU SAUTÉ LIHOU

PREPARATION TIME: *25 minutes*   **COOKING TIME:** *20 minutes*   **[M]**

Ingredients *(per 2 persons)*:

6–8 lamb's kidneys
150 g (6 oz) **Guernsey babaco**
50 g (2 oz) seasoned flour
25 g (1 oz) butter
200 g (8 oz) button mushrooms
15 g (½ oz) tomato purée
100 ml (4 fl oz) Muscadet (or
    other dry white wine)
1 pinch grated nutmeg
2 croûtons of fried bread
½ teaspoon parsley, chopped

Method:

1   Remove the membrane and core from the kidneys, wash under cold water and slice into 1 cm (⅓ in) slices.

2   Peel the babaco and liquidise the flesh. Squeeze the peel and save the juice.

3   Coat the kidney slices with the seasoned flour and fry in the butter. Add the mushrooms (sliced) and tomato purée and fry for 1 minute.

4   Add the wine, babaco and grated nutmeg, bring to the boil and simmer for 5 minutes until the sauce thickens.

5   Serve with heart-shaped croûtons of fried bread with the tips of the croûtons dipped in the sauce and then in the parsley.

Poultry and Game

BABACO KEBABS LA POIDEVINE

PREPARATION TIME: *20 minutes*   **COOKING TIME:** *20 minutes*

Ingredients *(per person)*:

1 fl oz (25 ml) oil
1 clove garlic
½ teaspoon English mustard
   powder
½ teaspoon tomato purée
Salt and milled black pepper
150 g (6 oz) chicken breast
175 ml (⅓ pt) chicken stock
50 g (2 oz) patna rice
15 g (½ oz) sultanas
8 washed button mushrooms
¼ each green and red pepper
1 slice 2 cm (¾ in) **Guernsey
   babaco**
½ teaspoon parsley, chopped

Method:

1   Place the oil, finely chopped
garlic, mustard, tomato purée,
salt and pepper in a bowl and
whisk well.
2   Skin the chicken breast and
cut into 2 cm (¾ in) cubes. Add
to the oil mixture and leave to
stand for 15 minutes.
3   Bring the stock to the boil,
add rice and sultanas and cook
for 15–20 minutes.
4   Wash the mushrooms and
peppers, cut into 2.5 cm (1 in)
squares and add to the chicken.
5   Cut the babaco into cubes
over the bowl of chicken to
catch the juices.
6   Put pieces of chicken, babaco
and vegetables on two kebab
skewers and grill, turning
regularly until cooked

(approximately 10 minutes).
7 Serve on a bed of rice sprinkled with the chopped parsley.

Note: Other meats may be substituted for the chicken.

BABACO MILL LANE

PREPARATION TIME: *15 minutes*   **COOKING TIME:** *45 minutes*   **[M]**

Ingredients *(per person)*:

1 × 200 g (8 oz) chicken breast
Salt and milled white pepper
15 ml (½ fl oz) oil
25 g (1 oz) butter
25 g (1 oz) plain flour
25 g (1 oz) tomato purée
25 ml (1 fl oz) Muscadet or
    other dry white wine
175 ml (⅓ pt) white chicken
    stock
150 g (6 oz) **Guernsey babaco**
6 fresh sage leaves, thinly sliced

Method:

1 Skin the chicken breast, season with salt and pepper and coat with a little oil.
2 Melt the butter in a pan, add the flour and cook for 2–3 minutes stirring constantly. Mix in the tomato purée, cook for a further minute, then add the wine and stock a little at a time to make the sauce. Bring to the boil and simmer for 30 minutes.
3 Peel the babaco and put the skin and any juices in the sauce. Cut the peeled babaco into cubes.
4 Strain the sauce, add the babaco and bring back to the boil.
5 Fry (or grill) the chicken until brown. Place in the sauce and simmer for 10 minutes, adding the fresh sage leaves.
6 Serve with savoury rice.

Note: Pork, veal or turkey can be substituted for chicken.

CHICKEN IN MUSTARD SAUCE

PREPARATION TIME: *20 minutes* **COOKING TIME:** *45 minutes* **[M]**

Ingredients *(per 2 persons)*:

150 g (6 oz) **Guernsey babaco**
2 × 150–200 g (6–8 oz) chicken breasts
50 g (2 oz) seasoned flour
25 g (1 oz) butter
25 g (1 oz) shallots
75 g (3 oz) Dijon mustard
100 ml (4 fl oz) Muscadet (or other dry white wine)
100 ml (4 fl oz) chicken stock
Salt and milled black pepper
50 ml (2 fl oz) cream
2 sprigs watercress

Method:

1 Cut the babaco into pieces and liquidise.
2 Dip the chicken breasts in the seasoned flour, heat the butter and brown the meat on both sides.
3 Remove the chicken from the pan and place in an ovenproof dish.
4 Fry the diced shallots in the butter, add the mustard, babaco purée, wine and stock, bring to the boil and pour over the chicken. Season with the milled black pepper, cover and place in an oven at 170°C (gas mark 3) for 30 minutes.
5 Remove the chicken and keep warm. Place the cooking stock on a high heat and reduce until it starts to thicken, add the cream, reboil, correct the seasoning and pour over the chicken.
6 Serve with rice poached in chicken stock and watercress.

EDWARDIAN CHICKEN

PREPARATION TIME: *20 minutes* **COOKING TIME:** *40 minutes* **[M]**

Ingredients *(per 2 persons)*:

150 g (6 oz) **Guernsey babaco**
100 ml (4 fl oz) plain yogurt

15 ml (½ fl oz) lemon juice
15 g (½ oz) tomato purée

1 clove garlic, finely chopped
15 g (½ oz) paprika pepper
Salt and milled black pepper
2 × 150–200 g (6–8 oz) chicken
  breasts
25 ml (1 fl oz) olive oil
1 tomato, skinned and depipped
6 mint leaves

Method:

1 Cut the babaco into pieces
and liquidise.
2 Blend the babaco pulp,
yogurt, lemon juice, tomato
purée, garlic, paprika, salt and
pepper well together.
3 Skin and trim the chicken
breasts and marinade in the
babaco mixture for 2–3 hours.
Remove and drain well.
4 Heat the oil until smoking
and quickly fry the chicken
breasts. Add the marinade and
bring to the boil. Pour into an
ovenproof dish and cover with a
lid.
5 Cook in an oven at 180°C
(gas mark 4) for 30 minutes.
6 Dice the tomato, shred the
mint leaves and add to the
chicken for the last 5 minutes of
cooking.
7 Serve with saffron rice or
steamed potatoes.

ISLAND CHICKEN

PREPARATION TIME: *30 minutes*   **COOKING TIME:** *20 minutes*   **[M]**

Ingredients *(per person)*:

1 slice, 2 cm (¾ in) **Guernsey
  babaco**
50 ml (2 fl oz) Muscadet (or
  other dry white wine)
100 ml (4 fl oz) white chicken
  stock
25 g (1 oz) butter
Salt and milled white pepper
150–200 g (6–8 oz) chicken
  breast, trimmed
15 g (½ oz) plain flour
25 g (1 oz) mushrooms, sliced
Puff pastry base 12 × 8 cm (5
  × 3 in) pre-baked (or croûton
of fried bread)
3 black grapes (halved and
  depipped)
25 ml (1 fl oz) double cream
½ teaspoon parsley, chopped

Method:

1 Take the end of a babaco
and scoop out the flesh
[approximately 25 g (1 oz)].
Blend with the wine and stock.
2 Lightly butter a small pan,
sprinkle with salt and pepper.

Place the chicken in the pan, cover with the wine, chicken stock and babaco mixture. Cover, bring to the boil, then simmer for 10 minutes. Remove from heat and cool.

3   Melt 15 g (½ oz) of butter in a small saucepan, add the flour to make a roux and cook (stirring all the time) for 1 minute until it has a sandy appearance. Add the cooking stock to the roux (over a moderate heat) in four stages, stirring constantly. Bring to the boil and simmer for 5 minutes. The sauce should be the consistancy of single cream (if not, add a little more chicken stock). Any juice from the babaco can also be added.

4   Fry the sliced mushrooms in a little butter and place in the centre of the babaco slice on top of the puff pastry base (or croûton of fried bread). Top with the cooked chicken breast and grape halves. Place in a hot oven and heat for 6–8 minutes.

5   Whilst the base is being heated, strain the sauce, adjust the seasoning, reheat and stir in the the cream. *DO NOT BOIL.*

6   Remove babaco dish from oven, place on a warmed serving dish, and coat with the hot sauce. Sprinkle with chopped parsley and serve.

RED COOKED CHICKEN

PREPARATION TIME: *20 minutes*   **COOKING TIME:** *10 minutes*

Ingredients *(per 2 persons)*:

2 × 200 g (8 oz) chicken
  portions
25 ml (1 fl oz) dry sherry
1 clove garlic, finely diced
10 g (⅓ oz) fresh ginger
25 g (1 oz) cornflour
Salt and milled black pepper
15 ml (½ fl oz) soy sauce
25 ml (1 fl oz) **babaco** juice
150 g (6 oz) **Guernsey babaco**
1 medium green pepper

1 medium red pepper
25 ml (1 fl oz) oil
125 ml (5 fl oz) chicken stock

Method:

1   Skin the chicken pieces, remove any bones and cut into 2.5 cm (1 in) pieces.

2   Blend the sherry, diced garlic, diced ginger, cornflour,

salt and soy sauce with the babaco juice. Add the chicken pieces and marinate for 1 hour.
3 Cut the babaco into 2 cm (¾ in) cubes.
4 Depip the peppers and cut into 2.5 cm (1 in) pieces.
5 Heat the oil in a wok (or deep-sided pan) and fry the chicken pieces for 1 minute. Remove and drain.

6 Reheat the oil and fry the peppers for 1 minute, add the chicken and chicken stock, bring to the boil and simmer for 5 minutes.
7 Add the babaco cubes, simmer for a further minute, stir in the marinade, reboil and check seasoning.
8 Serve with plain boiled long grain rice.

TROPICAL CURRIED CHICKEN SALAD

PREPARATION TIME: *15 minutes*

Ingredients *(per 2 persons)*:

150 g (6 oz) **Guernsey babaco**
200 g (8 oz) cooked chicken, diced
15 g (½ oz) spring onions
2 medium tomatoes
25 g (1 oz) red pepper, diced
100 g (4 oz) cooked long grain rice
100 ml (4 fl oz) plain yogurt
25 ml (1 fl oz) mayonnaise
1 teaspoon castor sugar
½ teaspoon curry powder
1 teaspoon parsley, chopped
Salt and milled white pepper

Method:

1 Cut the babaco into 1 cm (⅓ in) dice.
2 Toss the babaco, chicken, chopped spring onions, tomatoes (peeled, depipped and diced), red pepper and rice together in a bowl.
3 Whisk together the yogurt, mayonnaise, sugar, curry powder, parsley, salt and pepper.
4 Mix the babaco and yogurt mixtures lightly, cover and chill in a refrigerator for 1 hour before serving.

Recipe supplied by Sheila J. Gaudion

SOUTH AMERICAN DUCK

PREPARATION TIME: *30 minutes*   **COOKING TIME:** *3 hours*   [M]

Ingredients *(per 4 persons)*:

1 × 2 kg (4½ lb) duckling
Oil for frying
500 ml (1 pt) water
100 g (4 oz) onions
100 g (4 oz) carrots
3 cloves garlic
50 g (2 oz) seasoned flour
400 g (1 lb) **Guernsey babaco**
25 g (1 oz) butter
25 g (1 oz) plain flour
25 g (1 oz) tomato purée
1 teaspoon chilli powder
25 ml (1 fl oz) Malmsey
  (Madeira)
½ teaspoon parsley, chopped

Method:

1 Remove the breasts and legs from the duckling. Cut the carcass into pieces and roast in a little oil for ten minutes in a hot oven until brown. Remove, drain off the fat and place in a saucepan with the water, onions, carrots and garlic. Bring to the boil and simmer for 1½ hours. Strain (removing excess fat).
2 Dip the duckling pieces into the seasoned flour and fry to seal and brown. Place in an ovenproof dish, add the stock and 150 g (6 oz) of the liquidised babaco. Cover with a lid and braise for 1 hour in an oven at 180°C (gas mark 4). Strain the cooking liquid and remove excess fat.
3 Melt the butter, add the flour to make a roux, and cook for 1 minute until it has the appearance of wet sand. Add the tomato purée and chilli powder and cook for a further minute. Add the cooking stock from the duckling gradually, stirring all the time. Bring to the boil, pour over the duckling pieces and return to the oven for a further 30 minutes.
4 Cut the remaining babaco in half and then into thin slices. Add to the duckling for the last 15 minutes of cooking.
5 *To serve:* remove the duckling pieces, dress with the babaco slices and keep warm. Correct the consistency of the sauce, add the Madeira and pour over the duckling. Sprinkle with chopped parsley and serve with saffron rice.

BABACO AND TURKEY CASSEROLE

PREPARATION TIME: *20 minutes*   **COOKING TIME:** *1½ hours*   **[M]**

Ingredients *(per 4 persons)*:

200 g (8 oz) **Guernsey babaco**
800 g (2 lb) turkey flesh
100 g (4 oz) onions, diced
1 teaspoon dried sage
Salt and milled black pepper
250 ml (½ pt) water (or stock)
600 g (1½ lb) potatoes, peeled
25 g (1 oz) butter
15 ml (½ fl oz) cream
½ teaspoon parsley, chopped

Method:

1 Cut the babaco in half and then into thin slices.
2 Cut the turkey (dark and white meat) into pieces and mix with the onions, sage, salt and pepper.
3 In a casserole place alternate layers of turkey and babaco, add the water, cover and place in an oven at 170°C (gas mark 3) for 1¼ hours until the turkey is tender.
4 *Meanwhile:* cut the potatoes into even-sized pieces, place in salted water, bring to the boil and simmer for 20 minutes until cooked. Drain, cover with a lid and steam dry over a low flame for 2–3 minutes. Sieve (or mash with a potato masher), add the butter and cream.
5 Remove the casserole from the oven, top with the mashed potato (can be piped), return to the oven to brown, or glaze under a top grill.
6 Sprinkle with chopped parsley and serve with green vegetables.

PHEASANT SUZANNE

PREPARATION TIME: *40 minutes*   **COOKING TIME:** *3½ hours*   **[M]**

Ingredients *(per 4 persons)*:

1 × 1200 g (3 lb) pheasant
50 g (2 oz) onions, sliced
50 g (2 oz) carrots, sliced
50 g (2 oz) leeks, sliced
50 g (2 oz) celery, diced
1 sprig fresh rosemary
200 g (8 oz) **Guernsey babaco**
50 g (2 oz) seasoned flour
25 g (1 oz) butter
50 ml (2 fl oz) Scotch whisky
100 ml (4 fl oz) cream
½ teaspoon parsley, finely
   chopped

Method:

1   Remove the breast and legs from the pheasant, cut up the carcass and blanch (cover with cold water, bring to the boil and refresh under cold water).
2   Place the blanched carcass in a saucepan with 500 ml (1 pt) of cold water, vegetables and rosemary. Cover, bring to the boil and simmer for 1½ to 2 hours.
3   Keep four thin half slices of babaco for garnishing and liquidise the remainder.
4   Dip the pheasant pieces in the seasoned flour and fry in the butter, add Scotch whisky and set alight. Place into an ovenproof dish, add the babaco purée and strained stock, cover and braise in an oven at 170°C (gas mark 3) for 1½ hours.
5   Remove pheasant pieces and keep warm. Reduce the cooking liquid, add the cream, correct seasoning and pour over the pheasant pieces which have been decorated with the slices of hot babaco. Finish with chopped parsley.

BRAISED RABBIT WITH BABACO MARINADE

PREPARATION TIME: *30 minutes*   **COOKING TIME:** *2½ hours*   **[M]**

Ingredients *(per 4 persons):*

1 kg (2½ lb) rabbit
200 g (8 oz) **Guernsey babaco**
2 onions
2 sticks celery
100 g (4 oz) carrots
1 small leek
100 ml (4 fl oz) claret
50 ml (2 fl oz) oil
1 bouquet garni
25 g (1 oz) plain flour
25 g (1 oz) tomato purée
Salt and milled black pepper
1 teaspoon parsley, chopped

Method:

1   Cut the rabbit into suitable joints.
2   Peel the babaco and liquidise the flesh. Squeeze the skin and collect the juice.
3   Place the vegetables, wine, babaco pulp/juice, half the oil and the bouquet garni in a bowl, mix well, add the rabbit pieces (including the carcass) and marinate for 12 hours.
4   Heat the remaining oil, fry the rabbit pieces, remove and keep warm. Fry the vegetables, mix in the flour and cook for 2 minutes, add the tomato purée and cook for a further 2 minutes. Add the marinade a little at a time, bringing to the boil after each addition.
5   Add the rabbit, cover with a lid and braise in an oven 150°C (gas mark 2) for 2 hours (or until tender).
6   Remove the rabbit, strain the sauce and correct the consistency and seasoning. Place the rabbit in a serving dish, coat with the sauce and sprinkle with chopped parsley.

Vegetarian Dishes

BABACO NUT CRUNCH

PREPARATION TIME: *30 minutes*   **COOKING TIME:** *30 minutes*   **[M]**   **[V]**

Ingredients *(per person)*:

25 g (1 oz) mixed nuts
15 g (½ oz) wholemeal
  breadcrumbs
1 dessertspoon fresh mixed
  herbs, chopped
15 g (½ oz) vegetable margarine
15 g (½ oz) onion, chopped
25 g (1 oz) carrot, grated
15 ml (½ fl oz) vegetable stock
½ teaspoon yeast extract
½ teaspoon clear honey
1 dash lemon juice
1 × 2.5 cm (1 in) slice **Guernsey
  babaco**
Salt and milled black pepper

Method:

1   Grind the nuts until fine,

place into a bowl with the
breadcrumbs and mixed herbs
(using ½ teaspoon of dried
herbs if fresh are not available).
2   Melt the margarine in a
saucepan, add the onion and fry
until soft and light brown. Add
the grated carrot and cook for a
further 5 minutes. Add to nut
mixture.
3   Blend the stock, yeast extract
and honey together, add lemon
juice and mix into the nut
mixture. Season to taste.
4   Oil a suitable gratin (or other
ovenproof) dish and lay the
babaco slice in the centre.
5   Pile the mixture into the

centre cavity of the babaco, cover with kitchen foil and bake at 180°C (gas mark 4) for 15 minutes.

6 Remove the foil and bake for a further 5 minutes.

7 Serve hot with accompanying fresh vegetables.

Recipe supplied by Susan Farnham

BABACO CHEESE FONDUE

PREPARATION TIME: *15 minutes*   **COOKING TIME:** *20 minutes*   **[V]**

Ingredients *(per 4 persons)*:

150 g (6 oz) **Guernsey babaco**
1 clove garlic
200 g (8 oz) gruyère cheese
10 g (⅓ oz) cornflour
25 ml (1 fl oz) Calvados
Salt and milled white pepper
1 loaf French bread

Method:

1 Peel the babaco (saving any juices) and liquidise the flesh together with the clove of garlic. Squeeze the skin to remove any more juice.

2 Place the purée in a fondue pot and heat gently.

3 Grate the cheese and add to the babaco, stir gently until completely melted.

4 Slake the cornflour with the Calvados and stir into the babaco and cheese mix. Season with salt and pepper.

5 When the mixture is of a thick creamy consistency place over a low heat at the table and serve with the French bread (cut into cubes) as a fondue.

6 Serve with a tossed salad.

BABACO POLONAISE

PREPARATION TIME: *20 minutes*   **COOKING TIME:** *15 minutes*   **[M]**   **[V]**

Ingredients *(per 2 persons)*:

200 g (8 oz) **Guernsey babaco**
1 (size 2) egg
50 g (2 oz) white breadcrumbs

50 g (2 oz) butter
1 teaspoon parsley, chopped
Salt and milled white pepper

Method:

1 Cut the babaco in half lengthways and then into 1 cm (⅓ in) slices.
2 Lay the babaco slices 'domino' fashion onto the base of a shallow ovenproof dish.
3 Hard boil the egg, cool, grate the white and sieve the yolk.
4 Fry the breadcrumbs in half the butter until golden brown.
5 Mix the breadcrumbs, egg white, egg yolk and parsley together, season with salt and pepper and spread over the babaco slices.
6 Melt the remaining butter and dribble over the mixture. Bake in an oven at 170°C (gas mark 3) for 10 minutes.
7 Serve immediately.

SAVOURY BABACO CAKE

PREPARATION TIME: *40 minutes*   **COOKING TIME:** *45 minutes*   **[M] [V]**

Ingredients *(per 4 persons)*:

400 g (1 lb) **Guernsey babaco**
75 g (3 oz) butter
15 g (½ oz) white breadcrumbs
200 g (8 oz) Münster cheese
25 g (1 oz) castor sugar
½ teaspoon cinnamon
3 (size 2) eggs

Method:
1 Cut the babaco in half and then into 1 cm (⅓ in) slices.
2 Melt 25 g (1 oz) butter and stew the babaco slices for 5 minutes. Drain well.
3 Pre-heat the oven to 180°C (gas mark 4).
4 Oil a deep 2 litre (1½ pt) baking dish or mould and sprinkle with the breadcrumbs so that the whole surface is well covered.
5 Grate the cheese and mix with the sugar and cinnamon.
6 Separate the egg yolks from the whites and whisk the whites until stiff and peaked. Whisk the yolks until creamy and then gently fold the whites into the yolks.
7 Spread a ¼ of the egg mixture into the bottom of the prepared dish, add a ¼ of the babaco and then a layer of the cheese mix. Dot with small knobs of butter. Repeat the layering with the cheese and babaco and top with the egg mixture and dot with the

remaining butter.
8 Bake for 35 minutes.
9 Either serve from the dish or turn out onto a serving dish.

Note: This dish is also ideal to serve with grilled veal.

BABACO CLAFOUTIS

PREPARATION TIME: *40 minutes* **COOKING TIME:** *1 hour* **[V]**

Ingredients *(per 4 persons)*:

400 g (1 lb) **Guernsey babaco**
50 g (2 oz) butter
100 g (4 oz) strong flour
Salt and milled white pepper
3 (size 3) eggs
375 ml (¾ pt) milk
25 g (1 oz) parmesan cheese

Method:

1 Cut the babaco in half and then into 1 cm (½ in) slices. Drain (saving the juice) and lay in a shallow dish that has been well-buttered with 25 g (1 oz) of the butter.
2 Sieve the flour together with salt and white pepper into a bowl, make a well in the centre and pour in the beaten eggs.
3 Stir the eggs into the flour, allow to stand for 5 minutes then whisk in the milk until smooth. Cover and stand for ½ an hour in a cool place.
4 Add the babaco juice and parmesan cheese, re-whisk well and pour over the babaco slices.
5 Cut the remaining butter into pieces and place on top of the mixture.
6 Bake in a pre-heated oven at 200°C (gas mark 6) for 30 minutes then reduce the temperature to 180°C (gas mark 5) and cook for a further 20 minutes.
7 Serve immediately.

BABACO LA BELLENGERE

PREPARATION TIME: *15 minutes*　**COOKING TIME:** *15 minutes*　**[M] [V]**

Ingredients *(per person)*:

1 slice 1.5 cm (½ in) **Guernsey
 babaco**
1 large croûton fried bread
25 g (1 oz)) onion, diced
15 g (½ oz) butter
1 tomato, skinned and depipped
Salt and milled black pepper
25 g (1 oz) cheddar cheese
50 ml (2 fl oz) cheese sauce
½ teaspoon parsley, chopped

Method:

1　Place the slice of babaco
onto the croûton of fried bread
(cut to the size of the babaco
slice).
2　Fry the diced onion in the
butter until soft, add the
chopped tomato, season with
salt and pepper. Place the
mixture in the centre of the
babaco slice.
3　Slice the cheese into thin
wafers and place over the
babaco and filling. Bake at
180°C (gas mark 4) for 5
minutes until the cheese has
melted and the babaco heated
through.
4　Bring the cheese sauce to the
boil, add the chopped parsley
and seasoning. Pour over the
babaco, sprinkle with a little
grated cheese and brown under
the grill.

Note: The centre filling can be
changed to suit tastes. Other
fillings could include bacon,
mushrooms and a meat sauce
made out of the appropriate
stock.

BABACO FLORENTINE

PREPARATION TIME: *20 minutes*　**COOKING TIME:** *15 minutes*　**[V]**

Ingredients *(per person)*:

200 g (8 oz) fresh spinach
Salt and milled black pepper
100 g (4 oz) **Guernsey babaco**

15 g (½ oz) butter
50 ml (2 fl oz) béchamel sauce
¼ teaspoon English mustard
 powder

25 g (1 oz) cheddar cheese
1 teaspoon parmesan cheese
1 pinch paprika pepper

Method:

1 Wash the spinach leaves and remove the centre stems. Plunge into a saucepan of 100–125 ml (4–5 fl oz) boiling salted water, cover with a lid and simmer for 8–10 minutes. Refresh under cold water and squeeze out as much water as possible. Chop the spinach and season with salt and pepper.
2 Cut the babaco in half and then into 1 cm (⅓ in) slices.

Place in a pan with a knob of butter, cover with a lid and stew over a low heat for 5 minutes.
3 Heat the béchamel sauce, slake the mustard with a little milk, add to the sauce together with the cheddar cheese, and cook until the cheese melts.
4 Heat the butter in a pan, add the spinach and heat well. Place in a suitable heatproof dish in a nest shape. Place the drained babaco in the centre.
5 Coat completely with the cheese sauce, sprinkle with parmesan cheese and bake in a hot oven 230°C (gas mark 8) for 5 minutes. Sprinkle with paprika pepper and serve.

BABACO PROVENÇALE

PREPARATION TIME: *15 minutes* **COOKING TIME:** *20 minutes* **[M]** **[V]**

Ingredients *(per person)*:

50 g (2 oz) shallots, finely chopped
2 cloves garlic
25 ml (1 fl oz) olive oil
25 ml (1 fl oz) Muscadet (or other dry white wine)
2 tomatoes, skinned and depipped
½ teaspoon oregano, chopped
150 g (6 oz) **Guernsey babaco**
1 teaspoon parsley, chopped

Method:

1 Fry the shallots and finely chopped garlic in the oil in a covered pan until soft.
2 Add the wine and chopped tomatoes, simmer for five minutes and add the oregano.
3 Cut the babaco in half and then into 1 cm (⅓ in) thick slices.
4 Lay the babaco slices in a suitable ovenproof dish, coat with the sauce and cook for 15

minutes in an oven at 190°C (gas mark 5).
5 Remove, sprinkle with the chopped parsley and serve with savoury rice and hot garlic bread.

CURRIED BABACO GRANDE MARE

PREPARATION TIME: *20 minutes*   **COOKING TIME:** *15 minutes*   **[M]**   **[V]**

Ingredients *(per 4 persons)*:

400 g (1 lb) **Guernsey babaco**
50 g (2 oz) shallots, finely chopped
1 clove garlic, finely chopped
25 g (1 oz) butter
15 g (½ oz) green peppers, diced
5 g (¼ oz) Madras curry powder
25 g (1 oz) plain flour
250 ml (½ pt) vegetable stock
50 ml (2 fl oz) double cream
50 g (2 oz) mango chutney
1 teaspoon parsley, chopped

Method:

1 Cut the babaco into 1.5 cm (½ in) slices.
2 Fry the shallots and garlic in the butter, add the peppers and fry for 1 minute.
3 Add the curry powder, blend well and add the flour. Cook over a low heat for 2 minutes.
4 Gradually add the hot stock, stirring all the time. Bring to the boil, season, add the babaco slices and simmer for 10 minutes.
5 Add the cream, chopped mango chutney and chopped parsley.
6 Serve on a bed of plain boiled patna (long grain) rice with condiments.

Note: Ideally the babaco should be slightly under-ripe.

Suggested accompaniments:
Diced onion, diced tomato, diced cucumber, diced celery, diced apple, sultanas, lime pickle, poppadums, Bombay duck.

Recipe supplied by Peter R. Brierley

RENDEZVOUS DANS PARADIS

PREPARATION TIME: *30 minutes*   **COOKING TIME:** *15 minutes*   **[M]**   **[V]**

Ingredients *(per 2 persons)*:

1 medium aubergine
25 ml (1 fl oz) lemon juice
40 g (1½ oz) butter
25 g (1 oz) shallots, finely chopped
50 g (2 oz) red pepper, diced
50 g (2 oz) mushrooms, finely diced
150 g (6 oz) **Guernsey babaco**
2 medium tomatoes, skinned
200 g (8 oz) plain boiled patna rice
125 ml (¼ pt) double cream
Salt and milled black pepper
1 teaspoon parsley, chopped
1 medium kiwi fruit

Method:

1   Cut the aubergine in half lengthways. Poach gently in a little salted water and lemon juice for 6–8 minutes. When cooked place in cold water to cool.

2   When cold carefully remove the flesh with a sharp knife (taking care not to cut the skin) and dice into small pieces.

3   Clarify the butter (melt, allow to stand and carefully remove the oil from the sediment), then heat and fry the shallots, peppers and mushrooms. Add the babaco (which has been thinly sliced) and cook for 1 minute. Add one of the tomatoes (depipped and diced), rice and aubergine flesh, mix, add the cream and simmer to reduce by half. Season with salt and pepper and finally add the chopped parsley.

4   Place the mixture in the two aubergine skins and decorate the tops with alternative slices of peeled kiwi fruit and tomato. Brush with melted butter and bake at 190°C (gas mark 5) for 2–3 minutes until hot.

Recipe supplied by Peter R. Brierley

VEGETARIAN PILLOWS

PREPARATION TIME: *20 minutes*   **COOKING TIME:** *20 minutes*   **[M]**   **[V]**

Ingredients *(per 2 persons)*:

150 g (6 oz) **Guernsey babaco**
2 large cabbage leaves
25 g (1 oz) onions, diced
1 small clove garlic
25 ml (1 fl oz) olive oil
25 g (1 oz) red pepper, diced
50 g (2 oz) cooked (boiled)
   patna rice
50 g (2 oz) cheddar cheese,
   grated
125 ml (¼ pt) cheese sauce

Method:

1 Cut the babaco into 1 cm
(⅓ in) cubes.
2 Remove the central stalk of
each cabbage leaf, then plunge
the leaves into a pan of boiling
salted water and cook for 5–6
minutes. Remove and plunge

into cold water.
3 Fry the onions and garlic in
the oil, add the pepper and rice,
remove from heat and add the
babaco.
4 When mixture is cool add the
grated cheddar cheese (saving a
little for the topping).
5 Spread the cabbage leaves
onto a flat surface and place half
the stuffing in the centre of each
leaf. Wrap the ends of the
leaves around the stuffing to
form a parcel.
6 Place the parcels in a lightly
buttered, ovenproof dish, cover
with the cheese sauce, top with
the remaining grated cheese and
brown in a hot oven at 230°C
(gas mark 8) for 10 minutes.

PIMENTO LA SALINE

PREPARATION TIME: *45 minutes*   **COOKING TIME:** *15 minutes*   **[M]**   **[V]**

Ingredients *(per 2 persons)*:

2 large green peppers
1 small red pepper
150 g (6 oz) **Guernsey babaco**
25 g (1 oz) butter

25 g (1 oz) onions, diced
1 clove garlic, diced
50 g (2 oz) patna rice
50 ml (2 fl oz) water

½ teaspoon fresh thyme,
chopped
Salt and milled black pepper
25 g (1 oz) parmesan cheese

Method:

1 The green peppers should be
evenly shaped. Keeping the
flatest side as the base, cut out a
lid at the top and scoop out the
seeds. Trim the stalk. Wash
well.
2 Cut the babaco into pieces
and liquidise.
3 Melt the butter in a pan and
fry the diced onion and minced
garlic. Add the rice, fry for 1
minute and then add the babaco
pulp, water, thyme, salt and
pepper. Bring to the boil and

simmer until the rice is cooked.
4 Cut the red pepper into
strips 2.5 × 0.5 cm (1 × ⅕ in),
plunge into boiling salted water
and cook for 3 minutes. Drain
and add to the rice.
5 Stir in the parmesan cheese
and stuff the peppers with the
rice mixture. Replace the lid and
place in a buttered ovenproof
dish. Brush with a little melted
butter and bake in an oven at
200°C (gas mark 6) for 15
minutes.

Note: Whilst this has been
designed as a vegetarian dish,
diced cooked meats can be
added to the rice if required and
white meat stock can be used in
place of the water.

WEST COAST PIE

PREPARATION TIME: *30 minutes*　**COOKING TIME**: *25 minutes*　**[V]**

Ingredients *(per 2 persons)*:

300 g (12 oz) potatoes
1 egg yolk
50 g (2 oz) butter
Salt and milled black pepper
25 g (1 oz) onion, diced
50 g (2 oz) courgettes
1 medium tomato
200 g (8 oz) **Guernsey babaco**
1 teaspoon fresh sage, shredded

1 teaspoon parmesan cheese
1 teaspoon white breadcrumbs

Method:

1 Peel the potatoes and cook
in boiling salted water until
tender. Drain well, cover with a
lid and place over a low heat to

steam dry (shaking the pan to prevent sticking). Mash with a potato masher or pass through a sieve.

2 Beat the egg yolk and 25 g (1 oz) of butter into the potato, season with salt and pepper and keep warm.

3 Fry the onion in the remaining butter, add the sliced courgettes and cook for 2 minutes.

4 Skin and depip the tomato.

5 Cut the babaco in half and then into 1 cm (⅓ in) slices.

6 Add the tomato, sage and babaco to the courgettes, season with salt and black pepper and place in a pie dish.

7 Cover with the creamed potato (can be piped using a piping bag and star tube), sprinkle the top with the parmesan and breadcrumbs and bake in an oven at 200°C (gas mark 6) for 15–20 minutes until golden brown.

Note: Although this is a vegetarian dish, fish or shellfish can be added.

MAMA'S CANNELONI

PREPARATION TIME: *45 minutes*   **COOKING TIME:** *30 minutes*   **[M]** **[V]**

Ingredients *(per 2 persons)*:

6 canneloni tubes
200 g (8 oz) **Guernsey babaco**
2 medium tomatoes
400 g (1 lb) spinach
2 cloves garlic
50 g (2 oz) butter
25 g (1 oz) mushrooms, finely
    diced
25 g (1 oz) white breadcrumbs
Salt and milled black pepper
50 g (2 oz) onions, diced
25 g (1 oz) plain flour
100 ml (4 fl oz) Frascati (or
    other dry white wine).
25 g (1 oz) parmesan cheese
1 teaspoon oregano, chopped

Method:

1 Cook the canneloni tubes in boiling salted water for 15–17 minutes, drain and store in cold water.

2 Liquidise the babaco, skin, depip and liquidise the tomatoes.

3 Remove the centre vein from the spinach leaves and cook the leaves in a covered saucepan in a minimum of boiling salted water for 8 minutes, refresh under cold water. Squeeze the cooked leaves to remove excess water and chop finely.

4) Fry half the garlic in 25 g

(1 oz) of butter, add the mushrooms and spinach and cook for 2 minutes. Add the breadcrumbs, season with salt and milled black pepper. Allow to cool.

5 Fry the remaining garlic and onions in the remaining butter, add the flour and cook for 1 minute. Gradually add the wine, babaco and tomato pulp stirring all the time. Bring to the boil

and simmer for 5 minutes.

6 Stuff the canneloni with the spinach mixture and lay them neatly in a buttered ovenproof dish.

7 Add the cheese and chopped oregano to the sauce and pour over the canneloni. Bake in an oven at 200°C (gas mark 6) for 15 minutes until brown and bubbling. Serve immediately with parmesan cheese.

RISOTTO GUERNÉSIAIS

PREPARATION TIME: *15 minutes*   **COOKING TIME:** *25 minutes*   [M] [V]

Ingredients *(per 2 persons)*:

25 g (1 oz) butter
1 clove garlic, finely chopped
50 g (2 oz) onions, diced
25 ml (1 fl oz) olive oil
100 g (4 oz) long grain rice
375 ml (¾ pt) vegetable stock
50 g (2 oz) red peppers, diced
50 g (2 oz) green peppers, diced
50 g (2 oz) button mushrooms
Salt and and milled black pepper
100 g (4 oz) **Guernsey babaco**
25 g (1 oz) parmesan cheese
1 teaspoon parsley, chopped

Method:

1 Fry the garlic and onion in the oil until soft.

2 Wash the rice under cold water until the water runs clear. Drain and add to the oil. Cover

with a lid and cook over a low flame for 2 minutes.

3 Add the stock, bring to the boil and transfer to an ovenproof dish, cover and cook in an oven at 170°C (gas mark 3) for 15–20 minutes until all the stock has been absorbed.

4 Whilst cooking, fry the peppers and mushrooms in the butter, season with freshly ground black pepper.

5 Dice the babaco into 1 cm (⅓ in) pieces, add to the peppers. Cook for 2 minutes.

6 Remove the rice from the oven and gently fork in the peppers, mushrooms and babaco mixture together with the cheese and parsley. Serve immediately.

BABACO MIDFIELD

PREPARATION TIME: *30 minutes*   **COOKING TIME:** *10 minutes*   **[V]**

Ingredients *(per person)*:

50 g (2 oz) spaghetti
25 g (1 oz) onion, diced
2 cloves garlic
50 g (2 oz) butter (or oil)
150 g (6 oz) **Guernsey babaco**
50 ml (2 fl oz) cheese sauce
1 tomato, skinned and chopped
1 teaspoon parsley, chopped
25 g (1 oz) parmesan cheese
Salt and milled black pepper

Method:

1 Place the spaghetti in a pan of boiling salted water and cook for 15–17 minutes until soft but with a slight resistance to the bite. Drain and refresh under cold water. (The cooked spaghetti can be stored in a bowl of cold water until needed).
2 Fry the chopped onion and 1 garlic clove in half the butter (or oil) until soft, add the babaco (which has been peeled and diced) and cook for 5 minutes over a low heat stirring regularly. Add the cheese sauce and diced tomato and keep hot.
3 *To serve:* drain the spaghetti and plunge into a pan of boiling, salted water for 2 minutes. Drain and keep warm.
4 Melt the remaining butter (or oil) in a pan and fry the remaining diced clove of garlic. Add the spaghetti and parsley and stir to heat thoroughly.
5 Add the hot babaco mixture and parmesan cheese, mix well and serve with additional parmesan cheese.

Note: Though basically a vegetarian dish, meats can be added if desired.
The spaghetti may also be cooked in white meat stock and the flavour varied by adding other herbs

Savoury Snacks

PIZZA BABACO

PREPARATION TIME: *1 hour* COOKING TIME: *20 minutes*

Ingredients *(per 2 persons)*:

Dough:
125 ml (¼ pt) milk
5 g (⅕ oz) yeast
15 ml (½ fl oz) olive oil
200 g (8 oz) strong flour
1 pinch salt
Topping:
200 g (8 oz) **Guernsey babaco**
25 ml (1 fl oz) oil
2 cloves garlic, finely chopped
50 g (2 oz) onions, sliced
3 tomatoes, skinned and
   depipped
¼ teaspoon oregano, chopped
50 g (2 oz) mozzarella cheese
15 g (½ oz) parmesan cheese
12 black olives
6 anchovy fillets

Method:

1 *To make the dough:* Warm the milk to blood heat (34°C), add the yeast and oil. Sieve the flour and salt, mix in the liquid and knead to a smooth dough. Cover with a damp cloth and allow to prove until dough has doubled in bulk. Knead for a further 2–3 minutes when dough will be ready for use.
2 Pre-heat oven to 220°C (gas mark 7) and place the baking tray to be used in the oven.
3 Meanwhile cut the babaco in half and then into thin slices. Heat the oil and fry the minced garlic and sliced onion. Add the chopped tomatoes and oregano, cook for 2 minutes. Grate the mozzarella cheese.

4 Roll out the dough into a round base approximately 30 cm (12 in) diameter.
5 Remove the hot baking tray from the oven and quickly place the dough on the tray. Place the sliced babaco on the dough, spread with the tomato mixture, sprinkle with both the cheeses, dot with the olives and criss cross with the anchovy fillets.
6 Bake in the oven for 15–20 minutes until dough is golden brown.

HADDOCK AND BABACO TOASTIES

PREPARATION TIME: *20 minutes* **COOKING TIME:** *20 minutes* **[M]**

Ingredients *(per 2 persons)*:

150 g (6 oz) smoked haddock
250 ml (½ pt) milk
25 g (1 oz) butter
100 g (4 oz) **Guernsey babaco**
25 g (1 oz) plain flour
1 egg yolk
2 slices bread
Salt and milled black pepper
25 g (1 oz) cheddar cheese, grated
2 sprigs parsley

Method:

1 Poach the haddock in the milk with a knob of butter for 10 minutes. Remove and allow to cool.
2 Cut the babaco into 1 cm (⅓ in) cubes, allow to drain, saving any juice.
3 Melt the butter in a pan, add the flour to make a roux and cook over a low flame for 2 minutes until it has the appearance of wet sand. Add the milk a little at a time, beating well until all the milk is absorbed. Add the babaco juice and cook over a low heat for 5 minutes, stirring all the time (the sauce should be very thick). Remove from the heat and beat in the egg yolk.
4 Flake the haddock and add to the sauce together with the babaco. Correct the seasoning.
5 Toast the bread, heap the mixture on top, sprinkle with the grated cheddar cheese and brown under the top grill or in a hot oven. Top with a sprig of fresh parsley, serve immediately.

79

HAM AND BABACO SAVOURIES

PREPARATION TIME: *40 minutes*   **COOKING TIME:** *10 minutes*

Ingredients *(per 2 persons)*:

25 g (1 oz) butter
1 clove garlic, finely chopped
½ teaspoon paprika pepper
1 pinch cayenne pepper
200 g (8 oz) **Guernsey babaco**
100 g (4 oz) smoked ham
100 g (4 oz) strong flour
1 (size 1) egg
125 ml (¼ pt) milk
Oil for frying
25 g (1 oz) seasoned flour
1 teaspoon English mustard
   powder
100 ml (4 fl oz) béchamel sauce

Method:

1   Blend well the butter, minced garlic and peppers.
2   Cut the babaco in half and then into 2.5 × 1.25 cm (1 × ½ in) rectangles.

3   Thinly slice the ham and lightly spread one side of each slice with the butter mixture. Place a piece of the babaco in the centre (buttered side) and wrap so as to form a tight seal. Chill.
4   Sieve the flour and beat in the egg, leave to stand for 5 minutes and then whisk in the milk until smooth. Cover and allow to stand for 30 minutes.
5   Heat the oil to 175°C, dip the ham parcels in the seasoned flour and then in the batter and deep fry until golden brown. Drain on kitchen paper.
6   Serve with a light mustard sauce [1 teaspoon of English mustard added to 100 ml (4 fl oz) of béchamel sauce].

LETTUCE SAVOURIES

PREPARATION TIME: *30 minutes*   **COOKING TIME:** *35 minutes*   **[M]   [V]**

Ingredients *(per 2 persons)*:

4 large lettuce leaves
150 g (6 oz) **Guernsey babaco**

½ teaspoon Bovril
50 g (2 oz) white breadcrumbs
50 ml (2 fl oz) Muscadet (or

other dry white wine).
25 ml (1 fl oz) malt vinegar
1 teaspoon tarragon, shredded
6 black peppercorns
2 egg yolks
125 g (5 oz) butter
25 g (1 oz) tomato purée

Method:

1 Remove the centre vein from the lettuce leaves, plunge the leaves into a pan of boiling salted water and cook for 30 seconds. Remove, plunge into cold water and then drain.
2 Cut the babaco into 1 cm (⅓ in) cubes.
3 Blend the babaco, bovril and breadcrumbs and place a spoonful in the centre of each lettuce leaf. Wrap into parcels.
4 Butter an ovenproof dish and place the stuffed leaves on the

base. Add the wine, cover and cook in an oven at 180°C (gas mark 4) for 30 minutes.
5 Meanwhile place the vinegar, tarragon and peppercorns in a saucepan and boil until the vinegar has reduced by half. Strain into a bowl, add the egg yolks and whisk over a pan of boiling water until the mixture thickens.
6 Melt the butter and gradually whisk it, a little at a time, into the egg yolk mixture. When all the butter has been absorbed whisk in the tomato purée and keep warm.
7 Remove the lettuce leaves, lay into a hot serving dish, coat with the sauce and serve.

Note: If the sauce separates, whisk it slowly into a fresh egg yolk over a pan of hot water.

BABACO STROGANOFF

PREPARATION TIME: *20 minutes*   **COOKING TIME:** *10 minutes*   [M]   [V]

Ingredients *(per 2 persons)*:

300 g (¾ lb) **Guernsey babaco**
50 g (2 oz) onions, diced
25 g (1 oz) butter
50 g (2 oz) button mushrooms
1 level teaspoon paprika pepper
25 ml (1 fl oz) brandy
125 ml (¼ pt) cream
1 teaspoon parsley, chopped

Method:

1 Cut the babaco into strips 4 × 2 × 1.5 cm (1½ × ¾ × ½ in).
2 Fry the onion in the butter, add the sliced mushrooms and cook for a further minute. Add the paprika pepper and cook for 1 minute.

3 Add the babaco and stew gently for 3–4 minutes.
4 Heat the brandy in a ladle, flame and pour over the babaco.
5 When the flame has extinguished, add the cream, bring to the boil and simmer until it thickens (2–3 minutes).
6 Finish with the chopped parsley and serve with plain boiled patna rice.

GINGER BABACO WITH CRISPY SEAWEED

PREPARATION TIME: *20 minutes*   COOKING TIME: *20 minutes*   [V]

Ingredients *(per 2 persons)*:

200 g (8 oz) **Guernsey babaco**
2 large cabbage leaves (green)
25 g (1 oz) butter
1 teaspoon sesame oil
15 g (½ oz) fresh ginger
Oil for frying
Milled black pepper
1 large pinch grated nutmeg

Method:

1 Cut the babaco in half and then into 1 cm (⅓ in) slices.
2 Wash the cabbage leaves, remove the central vein. Roll the leaves into a tight 'cigar' shape and cut into fine strips. Dry well.
3 Melt the butter, add the sesame oil and lightly fry the grated ginger. Add the sliced babaco and stew for 5 minutes.
4 Heat the oil until it starts to smoke and deep fry the shredded cabbage for 1 minute. Remove the cabbage from the oil and reheat.
5 When the oil is once more very hot, return the cabbage and fry till very crisp. Remove from the oil and drain well.
6 Toss the cabbage with the milled black pepper and nutmeg. Place into a hot serving dish in the form of a nest and coat with the stewed babaco.
7 Serve immediately.

TREASURE TROVE

PREPARATION TIME: *30 minutes*   **COOKING TIME**: *30 minutes*

Ingredients *(per person)*:

200 g (8 oz) puff pastry
15 ml (½ fl oz) olive oil
100 g (4 oz) **Guernsey babaco**
25 g (1 oz) smoked bacon, diced
25 g (1 oz) onion, diced
25 g (1 oz) red pepper, diced
25 g (1 oz) green pepper, diced
25 g (1 oz) cucumber, peeled
  and diced
25 g (1 oz) mushrooms, diced
1 medium tomato
25 ml (1 fl oz) **babaco** dressing

Method:

1 Roll the puff pastry into a
rectangle 15 × 8 cm (6 × 3 in)
and 1 cm (⅓ in) thick. Cut, but
not completely through a centre
rectangle of 12 × 5 cm (8½ × 2
in) within the rectangle.
2 Brush the pastry with a little
beaten egg and bake in an oven
at 200°C (gas mark 6) for 20
minutes until well risen and
golden brown. Remove from the
oven and allow to cool on a wire
rack.
3 Cut the babaco into 1.5 cm
(½ in) cubes.
4 Heat the oil in a frying pan,
fry, in order, the bacon, onion,
peppers, cucumber, mushrooms
and finally the tomato (skinned,
depipped and diced). Remove
from the heat, add the babaco
and allow to cool.
5 Carefully remove the 'lid'
from the pastry case (vol-au-
vent) and discard the pastry
from the centre.
6 Toss the mixture in the
babaco dressing and fill the vol-
au-vent cavity with the mixture.
Replace the lid and serve.

Note: May be served hot or
cold. Omit the bacon for a tasty
vegetarian dish.

Vegetables

LEEKS WITH BABACO CREAM SAUCE

PREPARATION TIME: *30 minutes*   **COOKING TIME:** *1 hour*   **[M]   [V]**

Ingredients *(per 4 persons)*:

4 medium leeks
25 g (1 oz) butter
100 ml (4 fl oz) stock (or water)
Salt and milled white pepper
100 g (4 oz) **Guernsey babaco**
1 bayleaf
1 small onion
3 cloves
250 ml (½ pt) milk
25 g (1 oz) plain flour
15 ml (½ fl oz) double cream
1 teaspoon parmesan cheese
½ teaspoon parsley, chopped

Method:

1   Trim the leeks of their roots and poor quality leaves. Cut in half lengthways (enough root should be left to hold the half leek together). Wash well under cold water to remove any soil.
2   Plunge the leeks into boiling salted water and cook for 2–3 minutes until they are pliable. Remove and refresh under cold water.
3   Fold the ends of each half into the centre and lay them in a buttered dish. Cover with the stock (or water), season with salt and pepper, cover and cook in an oven at 150°C (gas mark 2) for 30–40 minutes.
4   Peel the babaco and liquidise the flesh. Squeeze the skin and save the juice.
5   Pin the bayleaf onto the peeled onion with the cloves, place in a saucepan, add the milk, bring to the boil, remove from heat and infuse for 15 minutes.
6   Meanwhile melt the butter, add the flour to make a roux and cook to a wet sand texture.

Add the milk a little at a time, then add the babaco pulp and juice. Bring to the boil and simmer for 20 minutes.
7 *To serve:* remove the leeks, drain well and lay in a serving dish. Strain the sauce, adjust the consistency with a little of the cooking liquid if necessary. Add the cream and pour over the leeks. Sprinkle with the parmesan cheese and parsley.

BABACO-STUFFED TOMATOES

PREPARATION TIME: *20 minutes* **COOKING TIME:** *10 minutes* [M] [V]

Ingredients *(per 4 persons)*:

150 g (6 oz) **Guernsey babaco**
15 ml (½ fl oz) olive oil
15 g (½ oz) butter
1 clove garlic, finely chopped
25 g (1 oz) onion, diced
4 large tomatoes
50 g (2 oz) white breadcrumbs
¼ teaspoon fresh sage, chopped
½ teaspoon parsley, chopped

Method:

1 Peel the babaco and dice the flesh.
2 Heat the oil and butter, fry the garlic and onion, add the babaco pulp and simmer until reduced by half.
3 Remove the top of the tomatoes (not the stalk end), retaining the lid, and scoop out the flesh.
4 Add the breadcrumbs and herbs to the babaco pulp and stuff the tomatoes with the mixture. Replace the lids.
5 Bake in a buttered ovenproof dish in an oven at 190°C (gas mark 5) for 10 minutes.

BAKED BABACO CREOLE

PREPARATION TIME: *20 minutes* **COOKING TIME:** *20 minutes* [M] [V]

Ingredients *(per 2 persons)*:

400 g (1 lb) **Guernsey babaco**
25 g (1 oz) butter

25 g (1 oz) onion, diced
1 medium green pepper

25 g (1 oz) celery, thinly sliced
200 g (8 oz) tomatoes
Salt and milled black pepper
50 g (2 oz) stuffed olives, sliced

Method:

1 Cut the babaco in half lengthways and then into slices of 1 cm (⅓ in). Butter an ovenproof dish and lay the slices 'domino' fashion along the bottom. Brush with melted butter, cover with kitchen foil and bake at 150°C (gas mark 2)

for 15 minutes.

2 Meanwhile place the remaining butter in a saucepan, cover and stew the onion, diced pepper and celery over a low heat for 10 minutes. Add the tomatoes (which have been skinned, depipped and diced), cook for a further minute.

3 Season the sauce, add the olives and pour the mixture over the cooked babaco.

4 Return to the oven (uncovered) for a further 5 minutes and serve.

ANDIAN POTATOES

PREPARATION TIME: *30 minutes* **COOKING TIME:** *20 minutes* **[M] [V]**

Ingredients *(per 4 persons)*:

300 g (12 oz) potatoes
300 g (12 oz) spinach
200 g (8 oz) **Guernsey babaco**
25 g (1 oz) cheddar cheese
15 g (½ oz) parmesan cheese
15 g (½ oz) white breadcrumbs
Salt and milled black pepper
50 g (2 oz) onions, sliced
15 g (½ oz) butter

Method:

1 Wash and scrub, but do not peel, the potatoes. Place in a saucepan, cover with salted water, bring to the boil and simmer until cooked. Remove

from the water and allow to cool. Peel and cut into 1 cm (⅓ in) slices.

2 Wash and remove the centre stem from the spinach. Cook the leaves in a minimum of boiling salted water for approximately 8 minutes. Refresh under cold water. Roughly chop and squeeze out the excess water.

3 Cut the babaco in half and then into 1.5 cm (½ in) slices.

4 Mix the cheeses, breadcrumbs and seasonings well together.

5 Lightly fry the onions in the

butter (do not brown).

6 Butter an ovenproof dish. Mix the potato and onion together and place in the bottom of the dish. Layer the babaco on top and cover with the spinach.

7 Cover the top with the cheese and breadcrumb topping and bake in an oven at 190°C (gas mark 5) for 20–30 minutes until topping is golden brown.

SAVOURY BABACO POTATO

PREPARATION TIME: *20 minutes*   **COOKING TIME:** *30 minutes*   **[M]** **[V]**

Ingredients *(per 2 persons)*:

300 g (12 oz) potatoes
Salt and milled black pepper
15 g (½ oz) butter
1 egg yolk
1 teaspoon tomato purée
200 g (8 oz) **Guernsey babaco**
1 large onion
25 ml (1 fl oz) olive oil
1 dash Tabasco
½ teaspoon parsley, chopped
1 teaspoon parmesan cheese

Method:

1 Peel and boil the potatoes in salted water. When cooked, drain, replace lid and steam-dry over a low heat until light and fluffy.

2 Pass the potatoes through a sieve (or mash with a potato masher until smooth and lump-free). Season with salt and pepper then beat in the butter, egg yolk and tomato purée.

3 Pipe the potato mixture with a star tube and piping bag into a nest-shape on a plate. Keep warm.

4 Cut the babaco in half and cut into thin slices. Cut the onion into thin slices and fry in the oil until soft. Add the babaco and fry for a further two minutes, stirring carefully. Add the tabasco and the chopped parsley.

5 Spoon the babaco mixture into the centre of the potato nest, dust with the parmesan cheese, brown under the top grill and serve.

Salads

BABACO DRESSING

PREPARATION TIME: *10 minutes*   [V]

Ingredients *(per 2 persons)*:

100 g (4 oz) **Guernsey babaco**
15 g (½ oz) shallot (or onion), diced
1 small clove garlic
25 ml (1 fl oz) olive oil
Salt and milled white pepper.
1 teaspoon parsley (or other fresh herb), chopped

Method:

1 Peel the babaco over a bowl to collect any juice that may be released and cut into pieces. (The skin can be squeezed in the hand to collect any remaining juice).
2 Place the babaco flesh, peeled and diced shallot, peeled and diced garlic clove, oil, salt and pepper into a blender and blend until thick and smooth.
3 Stir in a little chopped parsley (or other chopped herb) and use as a salad dressing.

Examples:
a) Potato salad: use chopped fresh mint.
b) Fish salad: use chopped fresh sage.
c) Cold meat salad: use chopped fresh sage and thyme.
d) Cucumber salad: use chopped fresh mint.

YULETIDE SALAD

PREPARATION TIME: *30 minutes* [V]

Ingredients *(per 4 persons)*:

200 g (8 oz) **Guernsey babaco**
200 g (8 oz) red cabbage
25 g (1 oz) walnuts
100 g (4 oz) cucumber

2 medium oranges
Dressing:
15 ml (½ fl oz) wine vinegar
25 ml (1 fl oz) olive oil
15 g (½ oz) cranberry sauce
Salt and milled black pepper
½ teaspoon caraway seeds
½ teaspoon celery seeds

Method:

1 Cut the babaco into 1 cm (⅓ in) cubes. Save any juice released.

2 Blend together the vinegar, olive oil, cranberry sauce, salt, black pepper, spices and any babaco juice.

3 Finely shred the cabbage and wash well.

4 Roughly chop the walnuts. Dice the cucumber into 1 cm (⅓ in) cubes.

5 Remove the zest and pith from the oranges and cut out the segments from the membranes.

6 Place cabbage, babaco, oranges, cucumber and walnuts in a salad bowl, add the dressing and mix well.

7 Serve as a side salad to accompany roast turkey, or as a starter.

BABACO AND CARROT SALAD

PREPARATION TIME: *20 minutes* [V]

Ingredients *(per 2 persons)*:

25 g (1 oz) sultanas
100 g (4 oz) carrot, grated
25 g (1 oz) shallots, finely chopped
200 g (8 oz) **Guernsey babaco**
5 g (¼ oz) curry powder
25 ml (1 fl oz) plain yogurt
½ teaspoon chervil, chopped

Method:

1 Soak the sultanas in boiling water for 15 minutes. Drain well and chop roughly.

2 Mix the sultanas, grated carrot and shallots well and place in suitable salad dishes.

3 Cut the babaco in half lengthways and slice into 0.5 cm (¼ in) slices.

4 Lay the babaco slices 'domino' fashion on top of the carrot mixture.

5 Blend the curry powder with the yogurt and spoon over the babaco, sprinkle with chopped chervil.

BABACO AND WATERCRESS SALAD

PREPARATION TIME: *20 minutes* [V]

Ingredients *(per 2 persons)*:

1 bunch watercress
200 g (8 oz) **Guernsey babaco**
2 slices bread
25 g (1 oz) butter
½ teaspoon Dijon mustard
25 ml (1 fl oz) olive oil
15 ml (½ fl oz) tarragon vinegar
Salt and milled black pepper
1 hard-boiled egg yolk
1 teaspoon chervil, chopped

Method:

1 Wash the watercress well and remove any very thick stems.
2 Cut the babaco in half and slice thinly. Save any juice.

3 Cut the bread slices into 1 cm (⅓ in) cubes and fry until golden brown in the clarified butter (butter melted and skimmed of its sediment). Drain on kitchen paper.
4 Blend the mustard, oil, vinegar, salt, pepper, hard-boiled egg yolk and babaco juice in a liquidiser and then mix in the chopped chervil.
5 Lay the watercress in a suitable dish. Neatly place the babaco slices on top and coat with the dressing.
6 Sprinkle with the croûtons and serve.

GUERNSEY COLESLAW

PREPARATION TIME: *20 minutes* [V]

Ingredients *(per 2 persons)*:

100 g (4 oz) savoy cabbage
50 g (2 oz) carrot
25 g (1 oz) onion
100 g (4 oz) **Guernsey babaco**
Dressing:
1 egg yolk

½ teaspoon English mustard powder
15 g (½ oz) castor sugar
1 clove garlic, diced
Salt and milled black pepper
50 ml (2 fl oz) babaco juice
25 ml (1 fl oz) olive oil

Method:

1   Finely shred the cabbage, peel and grate the carrot and finely dice the onion.
2   Slice the babaco into 2.5 cm (1 in) slices and add to the cabbage. Mix well together.
3   *For the dressing:* place the egg yolk, mustard, sugar, garlic, salt and pepper in a bowl with a teaspoon of the babaco juice. Blend well together. Whisk in the oil and remaining babaco juice.

4   Add the dressing to the cabbage mixture and mix gently.

5   Serve as a salad or starter.

ORIENTAL SALAD

PREPARATION TIME: *20 minutes*   **[V]**

Ingredients *(per 4 persons)*:

300 g (12 oz) **Guernsey babaco**
200 g (8 oz) bean sprouts
25 g (1 oz) shallots, finely chopped
25 g (1 oz) water chestnuts
25 ml (1 fl oz) oil
15 ml (½ fl oz) sesame oil
15 ml (½ fl oz) wine vinegar
15 g (½ oz) castor sugar
15 g (½ oz) fresh ginger, grated
1 clove garlic, diced
Salt and milled black pepper
25 ml (1 fl oz) **babaco** juice
Croûtons of fried bread

Method:

1   Dice the babaco into 1.2 cm (½ in) pieces. Save any juice.
2   Wash the beansprouts and place in a bowl with the finely diced shallots.
3   Dice the water chestnuts and add to the beansprouts.
4   Whisk together the oils, vinegar, sugar, ginger, garlic, salt and pepper with any babaco juice.
5   Add the dressing to the beansprouts and mix well.
6   Serve in salad dishes and garnish with small croûtons of fried bread.

BABACO CITRON

PREPARATION TIME: *20 minutes* **[V]**

Ingredients *(per 2 persons)*:

2 large lettuce leaves
1 teaspoon olive oil
2 teaspoons wine vinegar
Salt and milled black pepper
200 g (8 oz) **Guernsey babaco**
1 orange
1 lime
1 grapefruit
1 teaspoon dill, chopped
50 ml (2 fl oz) mayonnaise
2 slices of toast

Method:

1 Remove the centre stem from each lettuce leaf and discard. Shred the leaves finely.
2 Blend the oil and vinegar, season with salt and black pepper. Mix with the shredded lettuce.
3 Cut the babaco in half and then into 1 cm (⅓ in) slices.
4 Remove the peel and pith from the citrus fruits and cut out the segments between the membrane. Mix well together.
5 Mix the dill with the mayonnaise, season to taste.
6 Lay the lettuce on a serving dish and top with the babaco slices. Lay the fruit mixture on top of the babaco.
7 Coat with the dill mayonnaise and serve with hot fingers of toast.

ORANGE AND BABACO SALAD

PREPARATION TIME: *20 minutes* **COOKING TIME:** *10 minutes* **[V]**

Ingredients *(per 2 persons)*:

2 medium oranges
200 g (8 oz) **Guernsey babaco**
25 g (1 oz) butter
25 g (1 oz) shallots, finely
chopped
25 g (1 oz) white breadcrumbs
25 g (1 oz) ground almonds
1 teaspoon basil, chopped

Method:

1 Peel the oranges to remove the skin and white pith. Cut out the segments from between the membranes. Squeeze the membranes and collect the juice.
2 Cut the babaco in half and then into 1 cm (⅓ in) slices.
3 Melt the butter over a low heat and fry the shallots. Add the breadcrumbs and ground almonds and fry until golden brown. Add the basil, mix well and allow to cool.
4 Wash the lettuce well and shred finely. Toss in the orange juice and dress on a serving dish.
5 Lay alternate slices of babaco and orange on top of the lettuce and sprinkle the fried breadcrumb mixture on top.

SALADE EXOTICA

PREPARATION TIME: *15 minutes* **[V]**

Ingredients *(per person)*:

3 medium lettuce leaves
1 small tomato
1 small kiwi fruit
50 g (2 oz) **Guernsey babaco**
1 teaspoon oil
1 teaspoon wine vinegar
Salt and milled black pepper
1 teaspoon shallot, diced
25 ml (1 fl oz) single cream

Method:

1 Shred the washed lettuce leaves into strips.
2 Skin and depip the tomato, cut into cubes.
3 Peel the kiwi fruit and slice thinly.
4 Cut the babaco into half-slices and save any juices.
5 Make a vinaigrette with the oil, vinegar, salt and pepper, add the finely chopped shallot and mix with the lettuce.
6 Mix the tomato, babaco and kiwi fruit together.
7 Lay the lettuce on a serving plate (salad dish) and place the babaco mixture on top.
8 Stir the babaco juice into the cream and whisk until it starts to thicken. Spoon over the babaco mixture and serve.

Note: The salad can be served as an hors d'oeuvre or as an accompaniment to roast poultry, meat or game.

BABACO WITH CREAM CHEESE AND HERBS

PREPARATION TIME: *30 minutes*   [V]

Ingredients *(per 4 persons)*:

200 ml (8 fl oz) double cream
200 g (8 oz) curd cheese
15 ml (½ fl oz) olive oil
15 ml (½ fl oz) white wine
   vinegar
Milled black pepper
½ teaspoon chervil, chopped
½ teaspoon parsley, chopped
15 g (½ oz) chives, chopped
25 g (1 oz) shallots, finely
   chopped
1 clove garlic, finely diced
300 g (12 oz) **Guernsey babaco**

Method:

1   Whip the cream until stiff.

2   Combine the curd cheese, oil, vinegar, pepper, herbs, shallots and garlic, and fold into the cream.
3   Place the mixture in a muslin bag and stand in a plastic colander in a cool place to drain for 2–3 hours.
4   Cut the babaco in half lengthways and cut into 1 cm (⅓ in) slices.
5   Cut the lettuce into thin strips and dress onto a serving dish. Lay the babaco slices 'domino' fashion on the lettuce, and coat with the herb cheese. Serve with crispbread.

BABACO AND WALNUT SALAD

PREPARATION TIME: *10 minutes*   [V]

Ingredients *(per person)*:

150 g (6 oz) **Guernsey babaco**
25 g (1 oz) full fat soft cheese
1 tablespoon **babaco** juice
15 ml (½ fl oz) double cream

½ teaspoon tomato purée
Salt and milled black pepper
1 teaspoon chives, chopped
2 medium lettuce leaves
25 g (1 oz) walnuts

Method:

1 Cut the babaco in half and then into 1 cm (⅓ in) slices. Save any juice.
2 Blend the cheese with the babaco juice, cream and tomato purée. Season with salt and pepper, mix in the chopped chives. The dressing should be the consistency of double cream; if too thick, it may be thinned down with more babaco juice.
3 Wash the lettuce, remove the centre stems and dress onto a plate.
4 Lay the babaco neatly on the lettuce.
5 Roughly chop the walnuts, sprinkle over the babaco and coat with the dressing.

BABACO SALAD WITH HERB YOGURT DRESSING

PREPARATION TIME: *15 minutes* **[V]**

Ingredients *(per 2 persons)*:

300 g (12 oz) **Guernsey babaco**
2 large lettuce leaves
⅓ teaspoon sage, chopped
⅓ teaspoon tarragon, chopped
⅓ teaspoon parsley, chopped
⅓ teaspoon chervil, chopped
1 teaspoon lemon juice
50 ml (2 fl oz) plain yogurt
Salt and milled black pepper

Method:

1 Cut the babaco in half lengthways and then slice into 1 cm (⅓ in) slices.
2 Wash the lettuce leaves and remove the central stems.
3 Place each lettuce leaf on a suitable plate and dress with the babaco in a 'domino' fashion.
4 Mix the herbs, lemon juice and yogurt together, season with salt and freshly milled black pepper and pour over the babaco slices.

MARINATED BABACO WITH MINT YOGURT

PREPARATION TIME: *15 minutes* **[V]**

Ingredients *(per 2 persons)*:

200 g (8 oz) **Guernsey babaco**
½ teaspoon Tabasco sauce
15 g (½ oz) castor sugar
50 ml (2 fl oz) white wine
    vinegar
12 mint leaves
100 ml (4 fl oz) plain yogurt

Method:

1 Cut the babaco in half and then into 1 cm (⅓ in) slices.
2 Place the babaco slices in a bowl.

3 Blend the Tabasco sauce, sugar and wine vinegar, pour over the babaco and allow to marinate for 2 hours.
4 Wash the mint leaves, plunge into boiling water for 10 seconds, then into cold water. Drain and cut into fine strips.
5 Stir the mint into the yogurt and allow to stand for 1 hour.
6 Drain the babaco from the marinade. Lay neatly on a serving dish and coat with the mint yogurt.

Desserts

BABACO AND APPLE PIE

PREPARATION TIME: *15 minutes*   **COOKING TIME:** *25 minutes*

Ingredients *(per 2 persons)*:

100 g (4 oz) **Guernsey babaco**
15 g (½ oz) castor sugar
100 g (4 oz) dessert apples
150 g (6 oz) puff pastry
½ a beaten egg

Method:
1 Cut the babaco into 1.5 cm (½ in) slices and peel over a bowl to collect the juices. Squeeze any remaining juice out of the skin, stir the sugar into the juice.
2 Cut the flesh into 1.5 cm (½ in) cubes and add to the juice.

3 Peel, core and slice the apple. Add to the babaco, making sure it is coated with the juice. Leave to stand for 1 hour.
4 Place the fruit mixture in a pie dish and top with a crust of puff pastry (making a hole in the top to allow any steam to escape).
5 Brush the top with the beaten egg and bake at 200°C (gas mark 6) for 20 minutes.

Note: Other fruits such as bananas, pears or peaches may be used in place of the apples.

BABACO FLAN

PREPARATION TIME: *45 minutes*   **COOKING TIME:** *30 minutes*

Ingredients *(per 6 persons)*:

300 g (12 oz) **Guernsey babaco**

Flan case:
25 g (1 oz) castor sugar

100 g (4 oz) butter
1 (size 3) egg
150 g (6 oz) plain flour
Pastry cream:
2 egg yolks
50 g (2 oz) castor sugar
25 g (1 oz) plain flour
250 ml (½ pt) milk
2–3 drops vanilla essence
Glaze:
50 g (2 oz) apricot jam
50 ml (2 fl oz) water
15 g (½ oz) arrowroot

Method:

1 Cream the sugar and butter, add the beaten egg, fold in the sieved flour, roll out the pastry to make the flan case and bake blind (without filling). Allow to cool.

2 Cut the babaco in half and slice thinly (saving any juice).

3 Prepare the pastry cream:

whisk the egg yolks and sugar together until white, stir in the sieved flour. Bring the milk and vanilla essence to the boil in a thick-bottomed pan, whisk slowly into the egg yolk mixture. Place over a medium heat and bring to the boil stirring all the time. Remove from the heat, add the babaco juice then pour into the flan case and allow to cool.

4 When cool and set, decorate the top with the babaco slices in a 'fan' design.

5 Melt the apricot jam with the water, bring to the boil and add the arrowroot (mixed with a little cold water). Stir well until it reboils and cooks clear (15 seconds).

6 Coat the babaco with the apricot glaze, allow to cool and decorate with whipped cream.

GUERNSEY BABACO TART

PREPARATION TIME: *30 minutes*   **COOKING TIME:** *30 minutes*   **[M]**

Ingredients *(per 6 persons)*:

Pastry:
100 g (4 oz) butter
200 g (8 oz) plain flour
1 (size 1) egg
25 g (1 oz) castor sugar

Filling:
400 g (1 lb) **Guernsey babaco**
25 g (1 oz) butter
50 g (2 oz) castor sugar
50 g (2 oz) sultanas
1 level teaspoon cornflour
½ teaspoon cinnamon

Method:

1 *Prepare the pastry:* rub the butter into the flour to produce a breadcrumb texture. Beat the egg and sugar together, mix into the flour and gently form a smooth dough. Allow to rest.
2 Peel the babaco and cut into 1.5 cm (½ in) cubes. Squeeze the skin and retain the juice.
3 Melt the butter in a saucepan. Add the babaco, juice, sugar and sultanas, cover and cook over a low heat for 5 minutes.
4 Slake the cornflour with a little cold water and add to the babaco mixture. Bring back to the boil stirring until it thickens. Remove, add the cinnamon and allow to cool.
5 Line an 18 cm (7 in) flan ring with the pastry. Fill with the cold babaco mixture and cover with a pastry lid (seal the edges well and brush with a little beaten egg).
6 Make a small hole in the top to allow the steam to escape and then bake in an oven at 200°C (gas mark 6) for 30 minutes. Remove the flan ring for the last 10 minutes to allow the sides to brown.
7 Serve with custard sauce.

SOUTHERN BABACO PIE

PREPARATION TIME: *30 minutes* **COOKING TIME:** *30 minutes*

Ingredients *(per 4 persons):*

Pastry:
75 g (3 oz) unsalted butter
150 g (6 oz) plain flour
75 g (3 oz) castor sugar
1 (size 2) egg
1 teaspoon cold water
Filling:
50 g (2 oz) sultanas
400 g (1 lb) **Guernsey babaco**
25 g (1 oz) unsalted butter
25 g (1 oz) castor sugar
½ teaspoon ground cinnamon

Method:

1 Cover the sultanas with boiling water and allow to steep for 15 minutes. Strain.
2 *Prepare the pastry:* rub the butter into the sieved flour until it has the appearance of fine breadcrumbs. Dissolve the sugar in the beaten egg and water, add to the flour/butter mixture and gently mix to a smooth dough. Wrap in greaseproof paper and store in a cool place.

3 Cut the babaco in half and then into 1 cm (⅓ in) slices.
4 Melt the butter in a saucepan, add the babaco slices, cover and stew for 5 minutes. Add the sugar, cinnamon and sultanas. Remove from the heat and allow to cool.
5 Place the cool babaco mixture into a pie dish. Roll out the pastry to 1 cm (⅓ in) thickness and cover the pie dish. Decorate with a crimped edge, brush with a little beaten egg, sprinkle with castor sugar, make a small hole in the centre to let any steam escape and bake at 190°C (gas mark 5) for 20 minutes.
6 Serve with custard or cream.

BABACO STRUDEL

PREPARATION TIME: *1¼ hours* **COOKING TIME:** *40 minutes*

Ingredients *(per 6 persons)*:

Pastry:
200 g (8 oz) plain flour
1 (size 3) egg, beaten
25 ml (1 fl oz) oil
50 ml (2 fl oz) tepid water
Filling:
800 g (2 lb) **Guernsey babaco**
100 g (4 oz) sultanas
75 g (3 oz) melted butter
50 g (2 oz) cake crumbs, white
50 g (2 oz) castor sugar
½ level teaspoon cinnamon
1 teaspoon icing sugar
Sauce:
25 g (1 oz) castor sugar
100 ml (4 fl oz) water
1 level teaspoon cornflour

Method:

1 Place the sieved flour in a bowl, make a well in the centre and add the egg, oil and water. Mix into a dough with a fork. Turn out onto a floured board and knead for 15 minutes. Cover with an oiled sheet of greaseproof paper and rest in a warm place for one hour.
2 Peel and cut the babaco into slices and allow the juices to drain away (collecting them for the sauce). Blanch the sultanas until soft.
3 Roll the dough into a rectangular shape on a floured cotton teacloth until it is paper-thin and covers the cloth. Allow to rest for 20 minutes.
4 Brush the dough well with the melted butter and cover with the sliced babaco. Sprinkle with

the cake crumbs, castor sugar, sultanas and cinnamon.
5 Fold the edges (short sides) over the babaco approximately 3 cm (1 in) and roll 'swiss roll' fashion lengthways. Place on an oiled baking sheet and form into a horseshoe shape. Brush well with the remaining melted butter and bake in an oven at 180°C (gas mark 4) for 40 minutes. Remove, dust with icing sugar and serve hot or cold with sauce/cream.
6 For the sauce, boil the juices, skin, sugar and water together. Thicken with the cornflour (slaked with a little cold water). Bring to the boil, strain and serve.

CELTIC TORTE

PREPARATION TIME: *1 hour*   **COOKING TIME:** *10 minutes*

Ingredients *(per 6–8 persons)*:

4 (size 1) eggs
125 g (5 oz) castor sugar
125 g (5 oz) plain flour
200 g (8 oz) **Guernsey babaco**
25 g (1 oz) granulated sugar
50 ml (2 fl oz) **babaco** juice
10 g (⅓ oz) arrowroot
25 ml (1 fl oz) Kirsch
100 g (4 oz) flaked almonds
375 ml (¾ pt) double cream
6 glacé cherries
15 g (½ oz) angelica

Method:

1 Preheat an oven to 220°C (gas mark 7). Cut four 18 cm (7 in) diameter sheets of greaseproof paper, brush with oil and dust with flour. Place on baking sheets.
2 Whisk the eggs and castor sugar in a bowl over a pan of boiling water until the mixture is stiff (leaves the impression of the whisk for 2–3 seconds after the whisk is removed). Remove from the heat and whisk until cool.
3 Carefully fold in the sieved flour with a metal spoon, spread onto the greaseproof paper roundels and bake for 7 minutes. Remove from the oven and allow to cool.
4 Cut the babaco into 1 cm (⅓ in) cubes, place in a pan with the granulated sugar and babaco juice, bring to the boil and thicken with the arrowroot slaked with a little cold water. Boil for 30 seconds, remove and cool. Add the liqueur.
5 Toast the almonds in the

oven and cool. Whip the cream until peaked and stiff.

6 Remove the paper from the sponges and trim them. Pipe a ring of cream around the edges of 3 of the sponge rounds and fill the centres with the babaco mix.

7 Place the rounds on top of each other, finishing with the uncovered one. Spread with the whipped cream and cover the sides with the toasted almonds. Decorate the top with piped whipped cream, glacé cherries and angelica.

BABACO UPSIDE-DOWN PUDDING

PREPARATION TIME: *20 minutes*   **COOKING TIME:** *45 minutes*   **[M]**

Ingredients *(per 6 persons)*:

150 g (6 oz) butter
50 g (2 oz) soft brown sugar
400 g (1 lb) **Guernsey babaco**
100 g (4 oz) castor sugar
100 ml (4 fl oz) beaten egg
175 g (7 oz) self-raising flour
40 ml (1½ fl oz) **babaco** juice
15 g (½ oz) cornflour

Method:

1 Oil an 18 cm (7 in) round cake tin.

2 Cream 50 g (2 oz) of the butter with the soft brown sugar and spread over the bottom of the cake tin.

3 Cut the babaco in half and cut one of the halves into 5 mm (¼ in) slices. Lay these slices over the butter/sugar mixture, overlapping in a fan style.

4 Cream the remaining butter with castor sugar until light and fluffy, add the beaten egg a little at a time, beating well after each addition. Fold in the flour and bring to a dropping consistency with the babaco juice.

5 Spread the sponge mixture over the top of the babaco and bake in an oven at 180°C (gas mark 4) for 45 minutes.

6 Remove from the oven and turn out onto a serving dish.

7 Serve with a babaco sauce made by peeling the remaining half of the babaco and liquidising the flesh (squeezing the skin to obtain more juice). Bring the pulp and juice to the boil (with a little water if necessary) and thicken with the cornflour (slaked down with cold water). Reboil and serve.

GINGER BABACO BAKE

PREPARATION TIME: *15 minutes*   **COOKING TIME:** *30 minutes*   **[M]**

Ingredients *(per 4 persons)*:

1 × 800 g (2 lb) **Guernsey
    babaco**
25 g (1 oz) unsalted butter
125 g (5 oz) treacle
1 (size 1) egg
75 g (3 oz) wholemeal flour
10 g (⅓ oz) baking powder
5 g (¼ oz) powdered ginger

Method:

1 Cut the babaco in half
lengthways and remove the soft
centre from each half.
2 Lightly butter 2 sheets of
kitchen foil and wrap each of
the babaco halves separately.

Place them on a baking tray and
cook in an oven at 150°C (gas
mark 2) for 20 minutes.
3 Meanwhile cream the butter
and treacle together, beat in the
egg and fold in the flour, baking
powder and ginger which have
been mixed well together.
4 Remove the babaco halves
from the oven, open out and fill
the centres with the sponge
mixture.
5 Return to the oven (unwrapped) and bake at 190°C
(gas mark 5) for 30 minutes.
6 Serve hot with custard or
chocolate sauce.

ISLAND PUDDING

PREPARATION TIME: *20 minutes*   **COOKING TIME:** *25 minutes*   **[M]**

Ingredients *(per 2 persons)*:

300 g (¾ lb) **Guernsey babaco**
50 ml (2 fl oz) water
125 g (5 oz) castor sugar
1 level teaspoon cornflour
2 peeled kiwi fruit
100 g (4 oz) unsalted butter
2 (size 3) eggs

100 g (4 oz) plain flour
¼ teaspoon baking powder
1 teaspoon vanilla essence

Method:

1 Cut the babaco into slices
(saving any juice) and place in a

103

saucepan with the water and 25 g (1 oz) of the sugar. Bring to the boil and then thicken with the cornflour (slaked down with a little cold water). Add the sliced kiwi fruit, then pour into a pie dish and allow to cool.

2   Prepare the sponge by creaming the butter and remaining sugar together, add the beaten eggs a little at a time until smooth. Fold in the sieved flour and baking powder and a dash of vanilla essence (if the mixture is too stiff add a little milk). Spread over the babaco mixture.

3   Bake in a moderate oven 200°C (gas mark 6) for 20 minutes and serve with a vanilla sauce (or custard).

BABACO AND APPLE SLICE

PREPARATION TIME: *45 minutes*   **COOKING TIME:** *1 hour*

Ingredients *(per 4–6 persons)*:

150 g (6 oz) unsalted butter
150 g (6 oz) castor sugar
150 g (6 oz) plain flour
75 g (3 oz) ground hazelnuts
50 g (2 oz) ground rice
400 g (1 lb) cooking apples
300 g (12 oz) **Guernsey babaco**
50 g (2 oz) apricot jam
50 ml (2 fl oz) water
15 g (½ oz) arrowroot

Method:

1   *To make base:* cream 125 g (5 oz) of the butter with 50 g (2 oz) of castor sugar until light and creamy. Add flour, ground hazelnuts and ground rice and gently work smooth.

2   Line the paste into a 20 cm (8 in) flan case (ideally an oblong one). Bake blind (place a sheet of greaseproof paper filled with dried peas or beans in the centre of the flan case) in an oven at 170°C (gas mark 3) for 40–45 minutes. Allow to cool.

3   *To make the filling:* melt the remaining butter in a saucepan. Add the peeled, cored and sliced apples and half the babaco cut into pieces. Cover with a lid and cook gently over a low heat, stirring occasionally, until soft. Add the remaining sugar and allow to cool.

4   Place the babaco mixture in the flan case and decorate with the remaining babaco cut in half and then into thin slices.

5 Glaze with a little apricot glaze (melt the jam with the water, bring to the boil and thicken with the arrowroot slaked with a little cold water).
6 Decorate with whipped cream.

BABACO FRITTERS

PREPARATION TIME: *45 minutes*   **COOKING TIME:** *10 minutes*

Ingredients *(per 4 persons)*:

Batter:
100 g (4 oz) plain flour
1 (size 2) egg, beaten
50 ml (2 fl oz) milk
1 teaspoon oil
Sauce:
75 g (3 oz) **Guernsey babaco**
125 ml (5 fl oz) water
50 g (2 oz) castor sugar
1 teaspoon arrowroot (or cornflour)
4 slices 1.5 cm (½ in) **Guernsey babaco**
75 g (3 oz) plain flour
Oil for deep-frying

Method:

1 *To make the batter:* sieve the flour, make a well in the centre and add the beaten egg, stir and stand for 5 minutes. Add the milk and whisk until a thick, creamy consistency is obtained. Cover and stand for 30 minutes.

Before use add the teaspoon of oil and whisk well.
2 Heat the oil to 150°C.
3 Cut the babaco for the sauce into pieces and liquidise with the water. Place in a small saucepan. Add the sugar, bring to the boil and simmer for 5 minutes. Strain, return to the boil and thicken with the arrowroot (which has been slaked with a dessertspoon of cold water), making sure it reboils.
4 Slice the babaco and place in a bowl to allow excess juice to drain (10 minutes). Add the juice to the sauce.
5 Dip the babaco slices into a little flour, shaking off any excess. Dip into the batter and deep fry until golden brown.
6 Drain the fritters on absorbent paper and serve with the hot sauce.

Recipe supplied by Susan Farnham

BABACO BETTY

PREPARATION TIME: *20 minutes*   **COOKING TIME:** *1 hour*

Ingredients *(per 4 persons)*:

600 g (1½ lb) **Guernsey babaco**
150 g (6 oz) breadcrumbs
75 g (3 oz) butter
50 g (2 oz) soft brown sugar
½ teaspoon cinnamon
50 g (2 oz) golden syrup
125 ml (¼ pt) water

Method:

1 Cut the babaco in half lengthways and slice into 1 cm (⅓ in) slices.

2 Brown the breadcrumbs in a little butter and mix with the sugar and cinnamon.

3 In a deep, ovenproof dish place layers of babaco and breadcrumbs with knobs of butter, ending with a topping of breadcrumbs.

4 Dissolve the syrup in the water and pour over the dish.

5 Cook in a *bain-marie* (hot water bath) in an oven at 140°C (gas mark 1) for 1 hour.

6 Serve hot or cold with whipped, sweetened cream.

BABACO BRÛLÉE

PREPARATION TIME: *10 minutes*   **COOKING TIME:** *45 minutes*

Ingredients *(per 2 persons)*:

200 g (8 oz) **Guernsey babaco**
2 (size 2) eggs
15 g (½ oz) castor sugar
25 ml (1 fl oz) Kahlúa coffee
  liqueur
125 ml (¼ pt) single cream
25 g (1 oz) cakecrumbs
15 g (½ oz) ground almonds
50 g (2 oz) soft brown sugar

Method:

1 Cut the babaco in half and then into 1 cm (⅓ in) slices. Lay neatly in a buttered ovenproof dish.

2 Whisk the eggs, castor sugar, liqueur and cream together, strain and pour over the babaco.

3 Cook in a *bain-marie* (hot water bath) in an oven at 140°C (gas mark 1) for 40–45 minutes

until custard is set. Remove
from the *bain-marie*.
4 Mix the cake crumbs,

almonds and brown sugar,
sprinkle over the custard and
brown under the top grill.

BABACO CAMBRAI

PREPARATION TIME: *20 minutes*   **COOKING TIME:** *40 minutes*

Ingredients *(per 4 persons)*:

400 g (1 lb) **Guernsey babaco**
200 g (8 oz) plain flour
10 g (⅓ oz) baking powder
1 pinch salt
2 (size 1) eggs
50 ml (2 fl oz) milk
50 ml (2 fl oz) corn oil
75 g (3 oz) vanilla sugar
50 g (2 oz) butter
15 g (½ oz) castor sugar

Method:

1 Pre-heat the oven to 200°C
(gas mark 6).
2 Cut the babaco in half
lengthways and slice into 1 cm
(⅓ in) slices.
3 Sieve the flour, baking
powder and salt into a bowl.
Make a well in the centre.
Whisk the eggs, milk, oil and

vanilla sugar and stir into the
dry ingredients to form a stiff
batter.
4 Pour the batter into a 21 cm
(8 in) oiled tart tin and lay the
slices of babaco neatly on top.
(The babaco will sink slightly.)
Dot with knobs of butter and
sprinkle with the castor sugar.
5 Bake in the oven for 30–40
minutes until well risen and
golden brown. Test to see if it is
cooked with a skewer which
should come out clean.

Note: Vanilla sugar is produced
by standing a vanilla pod in
400 g (1 lb) of castor sugar for 2
weeks. Vanilla essence may be
used with castor sugar in lieu of
the vanilla sugar.

BABACO CRUMBLE

PREPARATION TIME: *15 minutes*   **COOKING TIME:** *40 minutes*   **[M]**

Ingredients *(per 4 persons)*:

Filling:
600 g (1½ lb) **Guernsey babaco**
25 g (1 oz) granulated sugar
Topping:
150 g (6 oz) plain flour
75 g (3 oz) unsalted butter
50 g (2 oz) castor sugar
¼ teaspoon cinnamon

Method:

1 Pre-heat the oven to 200°C
(gas mark 6)
2 Prepare the babaco by
cutting in half, then into 5 mm
(¼ in) slices. Place in a pie dish
together with any juice and
sprinkle with the sugar.

3 Sieve the flour and rub the
butter in until it has the texture
of fine breadcrumbs.
4 Gently mix in the castor
sugar and cinnamon, being
careful not to over-mix the
topping and turn it into dough.
5 Sprinkle the topping over the
babaco and level so that all the
babaco is covered.
6 Sprinkle the top with a little
castor sugar. Bake for 30–40
minutes. Serve with custard.

Note: One-third of the babaco
may be replaced by eating
apples.

BABACO JONATHAN

PREPARATION TIME: *20 minutes*   **COOKING TIME:** *40 minutes*   **[M]**

Ingredients *(per 4 persons)*:

100 g (4 oz) plain flour
10 g (⅓ oz) baking powder
1 pinch salt
300 g (12 oz) **Guernsey babaco**
40 g (1½ oz) butter
100 g (4 oz) castor sugar
1 (size 1) egg
25 ml (1 fl oz) maple syrup

Method:

1 Preheat an oven to 200°C
(gas mark 6).
2 Sieve together the flour,
baking powder and salt.
3 Cut the babaco in half
lengthways and slice into 1 cm
(⅓ in) slices.
4 Cream the butter and sugar

together until white and fluffy, add the egg and beat until smooth.

5 Fold in the sieved flour and gently mix to a smooth batter.

6 Lay the babaco slices in a lightly oiled dish, pour over the maple syrup and spread with the batter.

7 Allow to stand for 5 minutes, then bake for 35–40 minutes until brown and cooked.

BABACO CHEESECAKE

PREPARATION TIME: *20 minutes*   **SETTING TIME:** *2 hours*

Ingredients *(per 6 persons)*:

Base:
100 g (4 oz) digestive biscuits
25 ml (1 fl oz) Amaretto liqueur
50 g (2 oz) melted butter
Filling:
100 g (4 oz) **Guernsey babaco**
200 g (8 oz) full fat soft cheese
20 g (¾ oz) gelatine
50 ml (2 fl oz) milk
50 g (2 oz) castor sugar
125 ml (¼ pt) double cream
Decoration:
100 g (4 oz) **Guernsey babaco**
15 ml (½ fl oz) clear honey
50 ml (2 fl oz) double cream

Method:

1 Crush the biscuits and add the liqueur. Melt the butter and mix into the crushed biscuits. Place immediately into a 17 cm (7 in) flan ring (placed on a serving plate) and pat smooth.

2 Peel the babaco and liquidise the flesh together with any juice. Add to the cheese and blend well.

3 Dissolve the gelatine in the warmed milk together with the sugar.

4 Whisk the cream until thick. Add the milk mixture to the cheese and stir until it starts to thicken and set.

5 Fold in the cream and stir gently. Pour over the biscuit base and allow to set in a cool place (approximately 2 hours).

6 Decorate with thin slices of babaco and glaze with a little warmed clear honey. Pipe with whipped cream.

BABACO AND RAISIN BREAD

PREPARATION TIME: *20 minutes*   **COOKING TIME:** *1½ hours*   **[M]**

Ingredients *(per 6–8 persons)*:

150 g (6 oz) **Guernsey babaco**
75 g (3 oz) butter
150 g (6 oz) castor sugar
100 ml (4 fl oz) beaten egg
200 g (8 oz) self-raising flour
1 teaspoon bicarbonate of soda
100 g (4 oz) raisins
Grated zest of an orange
25 g (1 oz) ground almonds

Method:

1   Grease and line a rectangular loaf tin 21 cm × 11 cm (8 in × 4 in).
2   Peel the babaco and liquidise the flesh. Squeeze the skin and save the juice.
3   Cream the butter and sugar together until light and fluffy. Add the egg a little at a time, beating well after each addition. Sieve the flour and bicarbonate of soda and fold into the mixture.
4   Mix in the babaco, chopped raisins, orange zest and ground almonds.
5   Place in the tin and bake at 180°C (gas mark 4) for 1–1½ hours until firm to the touch. Turn out onto a cooling tray.
6   Leave to stand for 24 hours. Serve sliced with butter.

BABACO VICTOR HUGO

PREPARATION TIME: *15 minutes*   **COOKING TIME:** *20 minutes*

Ingredients *(per 2 persons)*:

2 × 2.5 cm (1 in) slices
  Guernsey babaco
25 g (1 oz) unsalted butter
25 g (1 oz) castor sugar
2 egg yolks
75 g (3 oz) ratafia biscuits
15 ml (½ oz) Amaretto

Method:

1   Place each of the babaco slices in small, buttered ovenproof dishes. Make the centre of each slice a little larger by cutting the flesh at a slight slant. Fill the base of the cavity with the flesh removed from the

sides.
2 Cream the butter, sugar and egg yolks together.
3 Crush the ratafia biscuits in a polythene bag with a rolling pin until they resemble fine breadcrumbs and add to the creamed mixture.

4 Combine the liqueur with the cream mixture.
5 Fill the babaco cavities with the creamed mixture and bake in an oven at 180°C (gas mark 4) for 20 minutes.
6 Serve in the dishes with whipped cream.

CHRISTMAS BABACO

PREPARATION TIME: *20 minutes*   **COOKING TIME:** *20 minutes*   **[M]**

Ingredients *(per 4 persons)*:

1 × 800 g (2 lb) **Guernsey babaco**
50 g (2 oz) cakecrumbs
200 g (8 oz) mincemeat
100 ml (4 fl oz) egg white
200 g (8 oz) castor sugar
12 glacé cherries, diced

Method:

1 Cut the babaco in half lengthways and remove the soft centres of both halves.
2 Mix the cakecrumbs and mincemeat together and place in the two halves.
3 Bake the babaco halves in an oven at 180°C (gas mark 4) for

10 minutes.
4 *Meanwhile:* whisk the egg whites with half the castor sugar in a grease-free bowl until stiff and peaked. Add the remaining sugar and re-whisk until it peaks once more.
5 Remove the babaco halves from the oven and heap (or pipe) the meringue on top of the mincemeat and babaco.
6 Sprinkle with the diced cherries, dust with a little castor sugar and return to the oven for a further 10 minutes until meringue has browned. Serve immediately with whipped cream.

MALTED BABACO

PREPARATION TIME: *30 minutes*   **COOKING TIME:** *30 minutes*   **[M]**

Ingredients *(per 4 persons)*:

300 g (12 oz) **Guernsey babaco**
50 g (2 oz) malt
25 ml (1 fl oz) water
50 ml (2 fl oz) **babaco** juice
50 g (2 oz) digestive biscuits
25 g (1 oz) unsalted butter
½ teaspoon arrowroot
100 ml (4 fl oz) double cream
25 g (1 oz) dark chocolate

Method:

1 Cut the babaco in half and then into 1 cm (⅓ in) slices. Place in a buttered ovenproof dish.

2 Dissolve the malt in the water and babaco juice, bring to the boil and pour over the babaco slices. Poach in an oven at 180°C (gas mark 4) for 15 minutes. Remove and allow to cool.

3 Crush the biscuits to a fine crumb (place in a plastic bag and pound with a rolling pin). Melt the butter and add the biscuit crumbs. Place the mixture in a flan ring which has been placed on a serving plate. Allow to set in the refrigerator.

4 Dress the drained babaco slices neatly on top of the biscuit base then remove the flan ring.

5 Put the cooking liquid on to boil, reduce and thicken with the arrowroot which has firstly been slaked with a little cold water. Reboil and coat the babaco slices.

6 When completely cool, decorate with the whipped double cream and the chocolate (which is either grated or in shavings using a vegetable peeler).

STEWED BABACO

PREPARATION TIME: *15 minutes*   **COOKING TIME:** *20 minutes*   **[M]**

Ingredients *(per 4–6 persons)*:

1 orange
800 g (2 lb) **Guernsey babaco**
100 g (4 oz) castor sugar
50 ml (2 fl oz) water
1 cinnamon stick
1 bayleaf
4 cloves

Method:

1   Remove the zest from the orange and cut into fine strips (julienne) 4 cm (1½ in) long. Squeeze out the juice and strain.
2   Cut the babaco in half and then into 1 cm (⅓ in) slices and arrange in an ovenproof dish.
3   Place the sugar, orange zest and spices in the water, bring to the boil and simmer for 5 minutes. Remove the spices.
4   Pour over the babaco and cook in a moderate oven 170°C (gas mark 3) for 15 minutes.
5   Remove from the oven, allow to cool, chill in the refrigerator.

Note: This can also be served as a breakfast dish.

BABACO WITH AUTUMN SAUCE

PREPARATION TIME: *20 minutes*   **COOKING TIME:** *20 minutes*   **[M]**

Ingredients *(per 4 persons)*:

300 g (12 oz) **Guernsey babaco**
50 g (2 oz) butter
100 g (4 oz) castor sugar
1 (size 3) egg
50 g (2 oz) ground hazelnuts
50 g (2 oz) cakecrumbs
200 g (8 oz) blackberries
100 ml (4 fl oz) water
15 g (½ oz) arrowroot

15 ml (½ fl oz) double cream

Method:

1   Cut the babaco into 1.5 cm (½ in) slices and remove the centre pulp.
2   Cream 25 g (1 oz) of butter with 50 g (2 oz) of castor sugar, beat in the egg and fold in the

ground hazelnuts and
cakecrumbs.

3 Lightly butter an ovenproof
dish and lay the babaco slices
flat on the bottom. Fill the
centre cavities with the hazelnut
mixture and bake in an oven at
150°C (gas mark 2) for 20
minutes.

4 Wash and pick over the
blackberries and place in a
saucepan with the remaining
castor sugar and water. Bring to
the boil and simmer until soft

(approximately 8 minutes).

5 Remove the blackberries
from the heat and pass
everything through a fine sieve
to remove the seeds. Return to
the saucepan, reboil and thicken
with the arrowroot which has
first been slaked with a little
cold water. Keep warm.

6 *To serve:* remove the babaco
and place onto a hot dessert
plate. Add the cream to the
blackberry sauce, being careful
not to boil, and serve.

BAKED STUFFED BABACO

PREPARATION TIME: *30 minutes* **COOKING TIME:** *20 minutes* **[M]**

Ingredients *(per 4 persons)*:

100 g (4 oz) sultanas
25 g (1 oz) unsalted butter
50 g (2 oz) castor sugar
100 g (4 oz) cakecrumbs
1 egg yolk
25 ml (1 fl oz) Grand Marnier
    liqueur
1 400 g (1 lb) **Guernsey
    babaco**

Method:

1 Place the sultanas in a
saucepan, cover with water and
bring to the boil. Simmer for 10
minutes, remove from heat and
leave to cool in the water
(approximately half an hour).

Drain well.

2 Melt the butter, add the
sugar and cake crumbs, remove
from the heat and add the egg
yolk and Grand Marnier. Pick
over the sultanas to remove any
stalks and add to the mixture.

3 Cut the ends off the babaco
and stuff the centre cavity with
the filling.

4 Butter a sheet of kitchen foil
and wrap the babaco so it is well
sealed.

5 Place in an oven at 190°C
(gas mark 5) for 20 minutes.

6 *To serve:* open at the table to
obtain maximum aroma. Serve
with ice cream or cream.

BABACO CRÊPES RUE DES PRÊS

PREPARATION TIME: *15 minutes*   **COOKING TIME:** *20 minutes*

Ingredients *(per 2 persons)*:

200 g (8 oz) **Guernsey babaco**
25 g (1 oz) castor sugar
50 ml (2 fl oz) water
15 g (½ oz) cornflour
Pancakes:
100 g (4 oz) plain flour
2 (size 5) eggs
125 ml (¼ pt) milk
Oil for frying

Method:

1 Cut the babaco into 1.5 cm (½ in) slices and peel over a bowl to collect any juice. Cut into cubes and squeeze the skin over the bowl to collect any remaining juice. Add the sugar and allow to stand.
2 Prepare the pancake batter by firstly sieving the flour, then adding the beaten eggs and mixing to a stiff batter. Stand for 5 minutes, add the milk and whisk for 1 minute. Allow to stand for 1 hour.
3 *To cook the pancakes:* oil a frying pan and heat until smoking. Whisk the batter and add 2 teaspoons of oil to the batter. Pour a little batter into the hot pan and swirl around to coat evenly. Cook for approximately 30 seconds, then turn the pancake over and cook the other side. Keep the cooked pancakes warm by placing flat on sheets of greaseproof paper (stacked) in a warming oven 110°C (gas mark ¼).
4 Drain the juice from the babaco cubes, place in a saucepan and bring to the boil. Thicken with the slaked cornflour, reboil and add the babaco cubes. Simmer for 2 minutes, then place a spoonful in each pancake, roll, decorate with a thin slice of babaco and serve with the remaining sauce.

HOT BABACO SOUFFLÉ

PREPARATION TIME: *30 minutes*   **COOKING TIME:** *40 minutes*

Ingredients *(per 6 persons)*:

400 g (1 lb) **Guernsey babaco**
15 ml (½ fl oz) Cointreau
50 g (2 oz) unsalted butter
50 g (2 oz) plain flour
125 ml (¼ pt) milk
1 teaspoon vanilla essence
4 (size 1) eggs
50 g (2 oz) castor sugar
100 ml (4 fl oz) water
25 g (1 oz) sugar
1 teaspoon arrowroot

Method:

1   Peel 300 g (¾ lb) of the babaco, cut into pieces and collect the juice, then purée (liquidise) the flesh. Squeeze the skin, retain the juice and add to the drained juice. Cut the remaining babaco in half and slice thinly.

2   Butter a 1½ litre (3 pt) soufflé dish, lay the sliced babaco on the base and sprinkle with the Cointreau.

3   Melt the butter in a saucepan, add the flour to make a roux and cook over a low heat (until a texture of wet sand is obtained).

4   Heat the milk and vanilla essence and add in stages to the roux (beating well after each addition). Add the babaco purée and cook for 5 minutes over a low heat.

5   Remove from the heat, cool slightly, beat in the egg yolks and sugar. Whisk the egg whites until stiff and peaked. Fold into the mixture and pour into the prepared dish.

6   Bake at 200°C (gas mark 6) for 40 minutes until golden brown and well risen.

7   Serve immediately with a sauce made from the babaco juice, water and sugar thickened with the arrowroot which has been slaked in a little cold water.

BABACO RICE PUDDING

PREPARATION TIME: *15 minutes*   **COOKING TIME:** *45 minutes*   **[M]**

Ingredients *(per 2 persons)*:

500 ml (1 pt) milk
75 g (3 oz) pudding (jap) rice
50 g (2 oz) castor sugar
50 g (2 oz) sultanas
15 g (½ oz) unsalted butter
1 cinnamon stick
25 ml (1 fl oz) double cream
200 g (8 oz) **Guernsey babaco**
50 g (2 oz) clear honey
50 ml (2 fl oz) water
½ teaspoon arrowroot

Method:

1 Place the milk, rice, sugar, sultanas, butter and cinnamon stick in a saucepan. Bring to the boil and simmer until all the milk has been absorbed and the rice is soft and cooked (30–40 minutes). Stir in the cream.
2 Cut the babaco in half and slice thinly. Save any juice.
3 Place the cooked rice in a lightly buttered serving dish and smooth the top.
4 Lay the babaco slices, overlapping neatly, on top and keep the pudding hot.
5 Dissolve the honey in the babaco juice and water and bring to the boil. Thicken with the arrowroot which has been slaked with a little cold water first. Bring back to the boil and cook for 30 seconds.
6 Pour the sauce over the babaco and serve.

Note: The pudding can be served hot or cold and the spice can be changed to suit taste, i.e. vanilla, ginger, allspice, etc.

BABACO AND FRANGIPANE BAKE

PREPARATION TIME: *15 minutes*   **COOKING TIME:** *20 minutes*   **[M]**

Ingredients *(per 2 persons)*:

200 g (8 oz) **Guernsey babaco**
50 g (2 oz) unsalted butter

50 g (2 oz) castor sugar
1 (size 3) egg

1 teaspoon plain flour
50 g (2 oz) ground almonds
15 g (½ oz) flaked almonds

Method:

1   Cut the babaco in half and
then into 1 cm (⅓ in) slices.
Place neatly in a buttered pie
dish (see also *note*).
2   Cream the butter and sugar
together until white and fluffy.
3   Gradually beat in the egg
until creamy.
4   Mix the flour and ground
almonds well and then gently

fold into the egg mixture.
5   Cover the babaco and place
in an oven at 180°C (gas mark 4)
for 15 minutes.
6   Remove the babaco from the
oven, coat with the frangipane
mixture, top with toasted flaked
almonds and glaze under a grill.
7   Serve hot or cold.

Note: This dish may be served in
a flan case if preferred. The
babaco cooked in the pie dish
first, then transferred to the flan
case.

BABACO CUSHIONS

PREPARATION TIME: *20 minutes*   **COOKING TIME:** *5 minutes*

Ingredients *(per 2 persons)*:

1 teaspoon orange zest
15 g (½ oz) icing sugar
25 g (1 oz) unsalted butter
150 g (6 oz) **Guernsey babaco**
4 thick slices white bread
2 (size 3) eggs
Oil for frying

Method:

1   Combine the orange zest,
icing sugar and butter.
2   Dice the babaco finely and
drain the excess juice.
3   Trim the crusts off the bread
and spread one side of each slice
with the butter mixture.

4   Place half the diced babaco
in the centre of two of the slices
(buttered-side) and place the
remaining slices (butter-side
down) on top, pressing the
edges firmly to form a tight seal.
5   Beat the eggs, strain and dip
the cushions into the egg to coat
each side.
6   Drain and fry in hot shallow
fat until they are golden brown
on each side.
7   Serve immediately with
cinnamon sugar (1 part
cinnamon to 12 parts castor
sugar).

BAKED BABACO-STUFFED APPLE

PREPARATION TIME: *20 minutes* **COOKING TIME:** *45 minutes* **[M]**

Ingredients *(per 2 persons)*:

2 large cooking apples
150 g (6 oz) **Guernsey babaco**
25 g (1 oz) unsalted butter
50 g (2 oz) brown sugar
25 g (1 oz) cakecrumbs
1 pinch powdered nutmeg

Method:

1 Core the apples and score the skin around the circumference of the apple.
2 Cut the babaco into pieces and liquidise, bring to the boil and simmer until reduced by half.
3 Melt the butter. Add the sugar, cakecrumbs, nutmeg and the babaco purée.
4 Butter 2 rounds of kitchen foil, place an apple in the centre of each sheet and then stuff the apples with the babaco filling. Wrap and place in a suitable ovenproof dish. Bake in an oven at 170°C (gas mark 3) for 45 minutes.
5 Remove from paper and serve with custard that has been flavoured with babaco purée [50 ml (2 fl oz) of purée per 250 ml (½ pt) of custard].

Note: If a microwave oven is used cook the apples unwrapped.

POACHED BABACO WITH SABAYON SAUCE

PREPARATION TIME: *15 minutes* **COOKING TIME:** *20 minutes* **[M]**

Ingredients *(per 2 persons)*:

250 g (10 oz) **Guernsey babaco**
50 ml (2 fl oz) water
125 g (5 oz) castor sugar

4 egg yolks
35 ml (1½ fl oz) Marsala
1 teaspoon Amaretto
½ teaspoon cornflour

119

Method:

1   Slice the babaco into 1 cm (⅓ in) slices and lay in a suitable ovenproof dish.

2   Bring the water to the boil, add 25 g (1 oz) castor sugar, dissolve and pour over the babaco. Cover with foil and poach in a moderate oven 150°C (gas mark 2) for 15 minutes.

3   Meanwhile place the egg yolks, remaining castor sugar, Marsala and Amaretto in a bowl and whisk over a pan of boiling water (*bain marie*) until about 4 times its original bulk. Keep warm.

4   *To serve:* remove the babaco, drain the cooking liquid and bring to the boil. Thicken with the cornflour (which has been slaked with a little cold water). Pour over the babaco slices.

5   Serve the babaco accompanied by the sabayon sauce and shortbread fingers.

SWEET BABACO KEBABS

PREPARATION TIME: *20 minutes*   **COOKING TIME:** *40 minutes*

Ingredients *(per 2 persons)*:

300 g (12 oz) **Guernsey babaco**
300 ml (¾ pt) milk
25 g (1 oz) unsalted butter
1 cinnamon stick
50 g (2 oz) castor sugar
100 g (4 oz) pudding (jap) rice
1 dessertspoon clear honey
25 g (1 oz) soft brown sugar
15 g (½ oz) angelica
12 glacé cherries

Method:

1   Cut the babaco into 2 cm (¾ in) slices, peel and squeeze the skin, saving the juice.

2   Cut the babaco into cubes and impale on skewers.

3   Bring the milk to the boil with half the butter, cinnamon stick and castor sugar. Add the rice and simmer until all the milk has been absorbed and the rice is cooked (approximately 25–30 minutes).

4   While the rice is cooking place the butter, honey, sugar and babaco juice in a saucepan and bring to the boil.

5   Place the skewered babaco onto a grill rack, brush with the honey mixture and grill for 8–10 minutes, brushing regularly with the mixture.

6 *To serve:* place the angelica and glacé cherries (cut into small pieces) in the rice and arrange on a serving dish. Top with the babaco and coat with the remaining honey/butter glaze.

BABACO AND ALMOND CLOUD

PREPARATION TIME: *20 minutes* **COOKING TIME:** *5 minutes*

Ingredients *(per 4 persons)*:

200 g (8 oz) **Guernsey babaco**
125 g (5 oz) castor sugar
1 knob of butter
3 egg yolks
5 egg whites
50 g (2 oz) ground almonds
25 ml (1 fl oz) Amaretto
4 slices **Guernsey babaco**

Method:

1   Peel the babaco and liquidise the flesh.
2   Mix the sugar with the egg yolks and whisk until creamy and thickened.
3   Preheat an oven to 220°C (gas mark 7). Lightly butter a shallow ovenproof dish and sprinkle with a little castor sugar.
4   Whisk the egg whites in a grease-free bowl until they are very stiff and firm.
5   Add the ground almonds (saving 1 level teaspoon for the topping) to the babaco pulp with the liqueur, mix well with the egg yolks and sugar.
6   Gently fold the mixture into the stiff egg whites, taking care not to allow the whites to collapse.
7   Place the mixture in the prepared dish, decorate with the babaco slices, sprinkle with the remaining ground almonds and bake in the oven for 5 minutes until golden brown.
8   Serve immediately.

SWEET OMELETTE EXOTICA

PREPARATION TIME: *10 minutes*   **COOKING TIME:** *5 minutes*

Ingredients *(per 2 persons)*:

100 g (4 oz) **Guernsey babaco**
1 small kiwi fruit
25 g (1 oz) castor sugar
½ teaspoon cornflour
3 (size 2) eggs
25 g (1 oz) unsalted butter
Icing sugar

Method:

1 Peel and cut the babaco into small cubes. Squeeze the skin to obtain the juice.
2 Peel the kiwi fruit and dice (cut the same size as the babaco).
3 Place the fruits, juices and sugar in a pan and bring to the boil. Thicken with the cornflour which has been slaked with a little cold water.
4 Beat the eggs well together. Preheat a poker or skewer over a flame to get it very hot.
5 Melt the butter in a large omelette pan and make the omelette. Before folding over, stuff with the fruit mixture.
6 Turn out the omelette onto a serving dish, sprinkle with the icing sugar and then brand in a lattice-work pattern with the hot poker (or skewer) to caramelise the sugar.

BABACO LES PLICHONS

PREPARATION TIME: *10 minutes*   **COOKING TIME:** *5 minutes*

Ingredients (per person):

2 cm (¾ in) slice **Guernsey babaco**
15 g (½ oz) unsalted butter
25 g (1 oz) castor sugar
25 ml (1 fl oz) **babaco** juice
25 ml (1 fl oz) orange juice
25 ml (1 fl oz) Kirsch

Method:

1 To prepare the babaco juice, slice the end off a ripe babaco and squeeze the juices into a bowl (the slice of babaco will also release some juice).

2 Melt the butter in a flambé pan (or frying pan) over a medium heat. Add the sugar and stir until dissolved. *DO NOT BURN*.

3 Add the babaco and orange juices a little at a time, stirring well with a fork.

4 Place the babaco slice in the sauce and cook for 2 to 3 minutes, basting with the sauce.

5 Sprinkle the babaco with a little castor sugar, add the the Kirsch and set alight. Allow flame to die down then serve.

Note: Other liqueurs or spirits can be substituted for the Kirsch such as white rum or Triple Sec but they must have a high alcohol content).

BABACO EN PAPILLOTE

PREPARATION TIME: *10 minutes*   **COOKING TIME:** *10 minutes*   **[M]**

Ingredients *(per person)*:

150 g (6 oz) **Guernsey babaco**
20 g (¾ oz) unsalted butter
15 g (½ oz) castor sugar
15 g (½ oz) flaked almonds
15 ml (½ fl oz) Cointreau

Method:

1 Cut the babaco in half and then into 5 mm (¼ in) slices.

2 Butter a sheet of greaseproof paper (or kitchen foil), cut out a disc of approximately 35 cm. (14 in) diameter. (If using the microwave you must use greaseproof paper).

3 Sprinkle one half of the buttered paper (or foil) with half the sugar and flaked almonds.

4 Lay the babaco slices along the top of the sugar and flaked almonds, sprinkle on the remaining sugar and flaked almonds and coat with the Cointreau.

5 Fold the uncovered half of the paper over the top of the babaco and twist the two ends together to form a seal.

6 Bake in a hot oven 240°C (gas mark 9) for 10 minutes.

7 *To serve:* bring to the table un-opened and then open in front of the diner. Crushed macaroons may be offered as an accompaniment.

BABACO FINGERS WITH PERNOD SAUCE

PREPARATION TIME: *30 minutes*   **COOKING TIME:** *30 minutes*

Ingredients *(per 2 persons)*:

300 g (12 oz) **Guernsey babaco**
50 g (2 oz) plain flour
3 (size 3) eggs
100 g (4 oz) white breadcrumbs
Oil for frying
Sauce:
100 g (4 oz) **Guernsey babaco**
100 ml (4 fl oz) plain yogurt
25 g (1 oz) unsalted butter
25 g (1 oz) plain flour
25–50 ml (1–2 fl oz) milk
25 ml (1 fl oz) Pernod
25 g (1 oz) castor sugar

Method:

1   Cut the babaco into strips
8 × 1.5 cm (3 × ¾ in). Drain
well in a colander and save the
juice.
2   *Meanwhile prepare the sauce:*
cut the babaco into pieces and
liquidise with the yogurt.
3   Melt the butter in a pan, add
the flour to make a roux and
cook over a low heat until it has
the appearance of wet sand.
Add the babaco and yogurt
mixture gradually, beating well
after each addition. After it has
all been absorbed, if it is still
too thick add a little hot milk.
Cook over a low heat for 20
minutes, stirring constantly.
4   When the babaco strips are
free of excess juice, dip them in
the flour, then in beaten egg and
finally in the breadcrumbs.
5   Heat the oil to 200°C and
deep fry the babaco strips until
crisp and golden brown. Drain
on kitchen paper and keep
warm.
6   *To serve:* strain the sauce,
add the Pernod and correct the
consistency with more hot milk
if necessary. Sweeten with the
castor sugar and serve with the
hot babaco pieces.

BABACO BORDELAISE

PREPARATION TIME: *10 minutes*   **COOKING TIME:** *25 minutes*   **[M]**

Ingredients *(per 2 persons)*:

100 g (8 oz) **Guernsey babaco**
Knob of butter
100 ml (4 fl oz) Sauternes
25 ml (1 fl oz) orange juice
25 ml (1 fl oz) **babaco** juice
25 ml (1 fl oz) clear honey
50 g (2 oz) seedless grapes

Method:

1 Cut the babaco in half and then into 1 cm (⅓ in) slices.
2 Butter an ovenproof dish, lay the babaco slices in the dish.
3 Place the wine, orange juice, babaco juice and honey in a saucepan and bring slowly to the boil. Stir well and pour over the babaco slices.
4 Place in an oven at 200°C (gas mark 6) for 10–15 minutes (until the babaco is cooked).
5 Remove the babaco slices and place on a serving dish. Return the cooking liquid to the saucepan and reduce until it starts to thicken, then add the grapes.
6 Pour over the babaco. Serve hot or cold.

BABACO IN RED WINE

PREPARATION TIME: *30 minutes*   **COOKING TIME:** *20 minutes*   **[M]**

Ingredients *(per 4 persons)*:

400 g (1 lb) **Guernsey babaco**
250 ml (½ pt) claret or other full red wine
1 stick cinnamon
1 small bayleaf
50 g (2 oz) castor sugar
2 pieces orange zest
15 g (½ oz) arrowroot
125 ml (¼ pt) double cream

Method:

1 Cut the babaco into 1.5 cm (½ in) slices. Save any juice.
2 Place the red wine, spices, sugar and orange zest in a saucepan, bring to the boil and simmer for 10 minutes. Strain, add any babaco juice.
3 Place the babaco slices in an ovenproof dish, add the red

wine and cover with kitchen foil. Cook in an oven at 150°C (gas mark 2) for 20 minutes.

4 Remove the babaco and allow to cool.

5 Bring cooking liquid to the boil and thicken with the arrowroot (which has been slaked with a little cold water). Allow to cool.

6 Place the babaco in a serving dish, coat with the red wine sauce and decorate with whipped cream.

GUERNSEY TRIFLE

PREPARATION TIME: *20 minutes* **COOKING TIME:** *5 minutes*

Ingredients *(per 4 persons)*:

300 g (12 oz) **Guernsey babaco**
200 g (8 oz) sponge cake
25 g (1 oz) raspberry jam
75 ml (3 fl oz) medium dry
   sherry
300 ml (12 fl oz) milk
25 g (1 oz) custard powder
25 g (1 oz) castor sugar
250 ml (½ pt) double cream
5 g (¼ oz) chocolate, grated

Method:

1 Cut the babaco into 1.5 cm (½ in) cubes.

2 Split the sponge cake (or sponge fingers) in half and spread with the jam to make a sandwich. Cut into slices and lay in the bottom of a dish.

3 Sprinkle with the sherry and add the babaco cubes. Mix gently together.

4 Bring the milk to the boil, add the custard powder slaked with a little cold milk, bring back to the boil and simmer for 1 minute. Add sugar to taste. Pour over the babaco and sponge. Allow to cool.

5 Whip the cream to a peak and pipe on top of the cold custard. Sprinkle with the grated chocolate.

SUMMER BABACO PUDDING

PREPARATION TIME: *20 minutes*   **COOKING TIME:** *5 minutes*

Ingredients *(per 6 persons)*:

600 g (1½ lb) **Guernsey babaco**
200 g (8 oz) blackberries
50 ml (2 fl oz) **babaco** juice
100 g (4 oz) castor sugar
150 g (6 oz) white bread
100 ml (4 fl oz) double cream
3 slices **Guernsey babaco**

Method:

1   Peel the babaco and collect any juice (squeeze the skin to obtain extra juice). Cut into thin slices.
2   Place the blackberries, babaco juice and sugar in a saucepan, bring to the boil and simmer for 5 minutes until soft but not in a pulp. Add the babaco and allow to cool.
3   Remove the crusts from the bread (which should be thinly sliced), cut into strips 5 cm (2 in) wide and then line a 75 cl (1½ pt) pudding basin so that each slice overlaps the preceeding one.
4   Pour in the babaco mixture and cover with more slices of bread.
5   Place a saucer on top of the pudding and a weight on the saucer, then store in the refrigerator overnight (12 hours).
6   To serve, turn out onto a serving dish and decorate with whipped cream and babaco slices.

Note: Other dark fruits such as blackcurrants and raspberries can be used in place of the blackberries.

SAUMAREZ CHARLOTTE

PREPARATION TIME: *40 minutes*   **COOKING TIME:** *10 minutes*

Ingredients *(per 6 persons)*:

50 g (2 oz) butter
15 ml (½ fl oz) sesame oil

6–8 thin slices white bread
15 g (½ oz) gelatine (leaf)

127

3 (size 3) eggs
250 ml (½ pt) double cream
200 g (8 oz) **Guernsey babaco**
200 g (8 oz) castor sugar
25 ml (1 fl oz) peach brandy
75 ml (3 fl oz) double cream
6 glacé cherries
3 thin slices **Guernsey babaco**

Method:

1   Clarify the butter (heat, allow solids to settle and separate from the oil), add the sesame oil to the butter oil.

2   Remove the crusts and cut the bread into strips 10 × 3 cm (4 in × 1¼ in) cutting one slice into a round to fit the bottom of a charlotte mould (cut into six segments). Heat the oil and fry the bread pieces until golden brown. Line the charlotte mould with the fried bread.

3   Soak the gelatine in cold water. Separate the egg yolks from the whites. Whip the cream.

4   Cut the babaco into pieces and liquidise.

5   Whisk the egg yolks and sugar over a pan of hot water until the mixture thickens. Add the softened gelatine and dissolve. Stir in the babaco pulp and peach brandy, until it starts to set.

6   Fold in the cream, whisk the egg whites in a grease-free bowl until very stiff and carefully fold into the mixture. Turn the mixture into the prepared charlotte mould and place in a refrigerator to set for 2 hours.

7   Turn out and decorate with rosettes of whipped cream, glacé cherries and thin slices of babaco.

BABACO SURPRISE

PREPARATION TIME: *15 minutes*   **COOKING TIME:** *2 minutes*

Ingredients *(per person)*:

2 cm (¾ in) slice **Guernsey babaco**
1 teaspoon Grand Marnier
10 cm (4 in) diameter sponge base
1 small kiwi fruit
50 g (2 oz) castor sugar

1 egg white
6 glacé cherries cut into strips
1 scoop vanilla ice cream

Method:

1   Peel the babaco (saving any

juice) and squeeze the skin, collecting any juice. Mix the juice with the Grand Marnier.

2 Place the sponge base on a serving dish, pour the liqueur and juice over the sponge. Place the babaco slice on top.

3 Peel the kiwi fruit, dice, and place the pulp in the centre of the babaco.

4 Preheat an oven to 200°C (gas mark 6).

5 Whisk half the sugar with the egg white until stiff then fold in remaining sugar and whisk until stiff once more. Add the strips of glacé cherries.

6 Place the scoop of ice cream on top of the babaco. Cover with the meringue, sprinkle with a little castor sugar and bake for 1–2 minutes in the hot oven until brown. Serve immediately.

Note: Other liqueurs can be used in place of the Grand Marnier. Other flavoured ice creams may also be used.

EXOTIC FRUITS GUERNSEY STYLE

PREPARATION TIME: *15 minutes*

Ingredients *(per person)*:

1 × 10 cm (4 in) diameter meringue shell
1 × 2 cm (¾ in) slice **Guernsey babaco**
1 small kiwi fruit, peeled
6 fresh strawberries
1 teaspoon Cointreau
25 g (1 oz) castor sugar
50 ml (2 fl oz) double cream
15 g (½ oz) macaroons, crushed

Method:

1 The meringue shell should be in the form of a 'nest' and perfectly dry. It should be large enough for the babaco slice to fit into snugly.

2 Peel the babaco and save any juices. Slice the peeled kiwi fruit thinly and slice 4 of the strawberries.

3 Mash the remaining 2 strawberries and add the babaco juice and liqueur. Sweeten to taste.

4 Whisk the cream until stiff and gently fold in the strawberry pulp.

5 *To serve:* line the shell base with the crushed macaroons then place the sliced kiwi fruit on top, followed by the babaco slice. Fill the babaco centre with the sliced strawberries and coat with the cream mixture, keeping a little to serve separately. Serve immediately.

Note: Other liqueurs such as Grand Marnier, Kirsch, or an Eau-de-vie may be used in place of the Cointreau.

BABACO FRENCH STYLE

PREPARATION TIME: *30 minutes*   **COOKING TIME:** *15 minutes*

Ingredients *(per 2 persons):*

200 g (8 oz) **Guernsey babaco**
50 g (2 oz) chestnuts
100 ml (4 fl oz) double cream
50 g (2 oz) castor sugar
50 g (2 oz) raspberry jam
50 ml (2 fl oz) water
15 g (½ oz) arrowroot
1 teaspoon milk chocolate,
   grated
2 mint leaves

Method:

1 Cut the babaco in half and then into 5 mm (¼ in) slices.
2 Peel and skin the chestnuts, cover with water, bring to the boil and simmer for 10 minutes until cooked through. Rub through a fine sieve.
3 Whip the cream and sugar until thick, blend in the chestnut purée.
4 Blend the jam and water, strain, bring to the boil and thicken with the arrowroot which has been slaked with a little cold water.
5 *To serve:* pour a little of the raspberry sauce into the well of a dessert plate. Lay the babaco slices in a fan shape over the sauce. Pipe a large rosette of chestnut cream at the base of the fan and sprinkle the grated milk chocolate over the cream.
6 A mint leaf can be used to add extra colour.

BATEAU DE BABACO AUX FRUITS D'ÉTÉ

PREPARATION TIME: *30 minutes*

Ingredients *(per 6–8 persons)*:

800 g (2 lb) **Guernsey babaco**
50 g (2 oz) small strawberries
50 g (2 oz) wild strawberries
50 g (2 oz) blackcurrants
50 g (2 oz) blueberries
50 g (2 oz) raspberries
50 ml (2 fl oz) Sauternes
6–8 mint leaves
1 egg white
15 g (½ oz) castor sugar

Method:

1 Cut the babaco lengthways to form a 'boat', making sure it sits firmly on its base.

2 Scoop out part of the centre leaving a little flesh on the skin.

3 Hull and wash the fruits and drain well. Marinate in the Sauternes for 30 minutes with the babaco flesh.

4 Place the marinated fruit into the centre of the babaco shell.

5 Decorate with frosted mint leaves (dipped in egg white and then in castor sugar).

6 Serve with cream.

Recipe supplied by Kevin Kennedy

BABACO FARCI AUX AMANDES

PREPARATION TIME: *20 minutes*

Ingredients *(per 6–8 persons)*:

90 g (3½ oz) unsalted butter
65 g (2½ oz) castor sugar
1 (size 2) egg
65 g (2½ oz) ground almonds
1 teaspoon pistachio nuts
800 g (2 lb) whole **Guernsey babaco**
2 medium kiwi fruit
6–8 fresh strawberries

Method:

1 Cream the butter and sugar together, blend in the egg, almonds and pistachio nuts.
2 The babaco should be a whole one. Cut off the ends and remove the soft centre.

3 Stuff the babaco centre with the creamed mixture and refrigerate for 2 hours to allow the filling to set.
4 *To serve:* slice in 1.5 cm (¾ in) slices and serve with sliced kiwi fruit and strawberries.

Recipe supplied by Kevin Kennedy

BABACO SOUFFLÉ

PREPARATION TIME: *30 minutes*　**COOKING TIME:** *20 minutes*

Ingredients *(per 4–6 persons)*:

300 g (12 oz) **Guernsey babaco**
20 g (¾ oz) leaf gelatine
3 (size 2) eggs
75 g (3 oz) castor sugar
250 ml (½ pt) double cream
50 ml (2 fl oz) double cream
2 slices **Guernsey babaco**

Method:

1 Tie a greaseproof-paper collar around a 1 litre (2 pt) soufflé dish so that it stands 8 cm (3 in) above the top.
2 Liquidise the babaco, bring to the boil and reduce to 50 ml (2 fl oz).
3 Soak the gelatine in cold water to soften.
4 Separate the egg yolks from the whites. Place the egg yolks, sugar and babaco pulp in a bowl and whisk over a *bain-marie* (pan of boiling water) until the mixture thickens (when the whisk is drawn across the top it leaves a trail which lasts for 3–4 seconds). Remove from the *bain-marie*, add the gelatine and continue whisking until the mixture is cool.
5 Whisk the egg whites until stiff. Whisk the cream, saving a little for decoration. When the mixture starts to set, fold in the cream and then gently fold in the egg whites.
6 Pour into the prepared soufflé dish, place in a refrigerator and allow to set (2 hours). Remove the paper collar and decorate with the whipped cream and babaco slices.

Recipe supplied by Roger Goodlass

MARASCHINO BABACO

PREPARATION TIME: *15 minutes*   **COOKING TIME:** *20 minutes*   **[M]**

Ingredients *(per 4 persons)*:

250 ml (½ pt) water
100 g (4 oz) granulated sugar
1 piece of orange zest
1 piece of lemon zest
400 g (1 lb) **Guernsey babaco**
  (small)
50 ml (2 fl oz) maraschino
  liqueur
50 g (2 oz) macaroons

Method:

1   Place the water, sugar and zests of a small lemon and orange in a pan, bring to the boil and simmer for 5 minutes. Strain.

2   Cut the babaco into 1.5 cm (½ in) slices, lay in a suitable ovenproof dish and cover with the syrup.
3   Cover and place the babaco in an oven 180°C (gas mark 4) for 10 minutes.
4   Remove from the oven, strain syrup into a saucepan and rapidly boil to reduce by half.
5   Allow to cool. Add the maraschino liqueur.
6   Place the cold babaco in a suitable serving dish, coat with the syrup and serve with macaroons.

TIPSY BABACO

PREPARATION TIME: *15 minutes*

Ingredients *(per 2 persons)*:

1 small lemon
25 ml (1 fl oz) cognac brandy
25 ml (1 fl oz) dry sherry
75 g (3 oz) castor sugar
250 ml (½ pt) double cream
100 ml (4 fl oz) **Guernsey babaco**
  purée
1 teaspoon milk chocolate,
  grated

Method:

1   Grate the zest from the lemon and then squeeze the juice.
2   Combine the lemon zest, juice, brandy and sherry and stand for 1 hour.
3   Stir in the sugar until dissolved.
4   Add cream and whisk until it

thickens.
5   Fold in the babaco purée,
pour into goblets and chill for
2–3 hours in a refrigerator.

6   Decorate with a rosette of
whipped cream and grated
chocolate.

BABACOMANGO

PREPARATION TIME: *20 minutes*

Ingredients *(per 4 persons)*:

400 g (1 lb) **Guernsey babaco**
1 ripe mango
25 g (1 oz) castor sugar
100 ml (4 fl oz) Cointreau or
   white rum
250 ml (10 fl oz) double cream

Method:

1   Keep 4 slices of babaco for
decoration and cut the
remainder of the babaco into
small pieces and place in a bowl.
2   Peel the mango and remove
the stone, cut into pieces and

add to the babaco.
3   Sprinkle the fruit with the
sugar and liqueur and allow to
stand for 30 minutes.
4   Whip the cream until stiff.
5   Liquidise the fruit and fold
into the cream.
6   Spoon the mixture into
serving coupes or dishes and
place in the refrigerator for 2–3
hours, until set.
7   Decorate with the babaco
slices and serve with sponge
fingers.

Recipe supplied by Patricia Savill

BABACO AND KIWI JELLY

PREPARATION TIME: *30 minutes* **Cooking time:** *10 minutes*

Ingredients *(per 4 persons)*:

600 g (1½ lb) **Guernsey babaco**
Water

50 g (2 oz) castor sugar
2 egg whites

25 g (1 oz) gelatine (leaf)
1–2 drops green food colouring
2 medium kiwi fruit
100 ml (4 fl oz) double cream

Method:

1 Thinly slice 100 g (4 oz) of the babaco for decoration.
2 Cut the remaining babaco into pieces and liquidise the flesh. Strain through a fine muslin (the pulp can be used for other recipes).
3 Make the juice up to 400 ml (1 pt) with water, add the sugar and slowly bring to the boil. Whisk in the egg whites and allow to simmer for 5 minutes. Remove from the heat and allow to cool slightly.
4 Strain carefully through a jelly bag or fine muslin.

5 Soak the gelatine and dissolve in the warm juice. Add 1–2 drops of green colouring to obtain a light pastel green colour.
6 Place a little of the liquid jelly in the base of a mould and decorate with slices of babaco and peeled sliced kiwi fruit. Place in the refrigerator to set.
7 When set, place the remaining jelly in the mould and return to the refrigerator to set (2 hours).
8 Turn out by dipping the outside of the mould in a bath of hot water for 2–3 seconds. Decorate with whipped cream and slices of fruit.

Note: Powdered (crystal) gelatine may be used following the manufacturer's instructions.

BABACO RUMTOPF

PREPARATION TIME: *1½ hours.*

Ingredients *(per 8 persons)*:

800 g (2 lb) **Guernsey babaco**
400 g (1 lb) castor sugar
750 ml (1¼ pt) white rum

Method:

1 Cut the babaco into four pieces lengthways and then into 2.5 cm (1 in) slices.

2 Place the babaco in a bowl and sprinkle with the castor sugar. Allow to stand for 1 hour.
3 Place the babaco, sugar and any juices in the rumtopf (see *note*), packing well.
4 Cover with the rum (more or less may be required according

to the size of the pot and how well the babaco is packed).

5 Make sure the babaco pieces are completely immersed in the rum (if not place a weighted saucer on top) and cover with clingfilm or foil.

6 The fruit will be ready from approximately 6 weeks and will keep for months.

Note: Specially made rumtopfs (also known as rumpots) can be purchased or a wide-mouthed crock/glass jar can be used.

Any amount of babaco can be used but the recipe must be adhered to.

Other fruits can be added as part of the weight of babaco.

Brandy, vodka or gin can be used in place of the rum if required.

BABACO BRAZILIAN

PREPARATION TIME: *30 minutes*   COOKING TIME: *10 minutes* [M]

Ingredients *(per 4 persons)*:

400 g (1 lb) **Guernsey babaco**
15 g (½ oz) unsalted butter
50 g (2 oz) soft brown sugar
125 ml (¼ pt) **babaco** juice
25 ml (1 fl oz) white rum
250 ml (½ pt) coffee ice cream
1 sponge flan case
100 ml (4 fl oz) double cream
8 walnut halves

Method:

1 Cut the babaco in half and then into 2 cm (¾ in) slices and lay in an ovenproof dish.
2 Melt the butter, add the sugar and babaco juice, bring to the boil and pour over the babaco slices. Cover, place in a hot oven 200°C (gas mark 6) and cook for 10 minutes. Remove from the oven and allow to cool.
3 When the babaco is cool, remove from the cooking liquid and refrigerate. Bring the cooking liquid to the boil and reduce to a syrup. Allow to cool, add the rum and place in the refrigerator.
4 Spread the ice cream onto the base of the sponge flan base. Dress with the babaco slices, coat the slices with the liquid and rum glaze.
5 Decorate with whipped double cream and walnut halves.

ISLAND BOUNTY

PREPARATION TIME: *30 minutes*   **COOKING TIME:** *10 minutes*

Ingredients *(per 4 persons)*:

150 g (6 oz) **Guernsey babaco**
3 (size 2) eggs, separated
200 g (8 oz) cheese curds
125 g (5 oz) kiwi fruit yogurt
75 g (3 oz) castor sugar
25 g (1 oz) gelatine (leaf)
65 ml (2½ fl oz) water
125 ml (¼ pt) double cream
1 medium kiwi fruit

Method:

1   Peel the babaco and liquidise the flesh together with the egg yolks, curds, yogurt and castor sugar. Place over a bowl of hot water (*bain-marie*) and whisk until the mixture thickens.

2   Remove from the *bain-marie* and whisk until cool.

3   Dissolve the gelatine in the warmed water and add to the mixture.

4   Whip the cream and fold into the cold mixture.

5   Whisk the egg whites until stiff and peaked, and gently fold into the mixture. Pour into individual glasses or a large bowl and place in the refrigerator to set.

6   Decorate with the peeled, sliced kiwi fruit and whipped cream.

Recipe supplied by Janet Bisson

BABACO SNOW

PREPARATION TIME: *30 minutes*   **COOKING TIME:** *15 minutes*

Ingredients *(per 4 persons)*:

400 g (1 lb) **Guernsey babaco**
2 (size 3) eggs
20 g (¾ oz) gelatine (leaf)
50 g (2 oz) castor sugar
6 glacé cherries
1 in (2.5 cm) piece of angelica

Method:

1   Peel the babaco and liquidise the flesh. Squeeze the skin and save the juice.

2   Separate the egg yolks from the whites.

3   Heat 100 ml (4 fl oz) of the

babaco pulp and juice and dissolve the gelatine in it.

4 Whisk the egg yolks and sugar over a pan of boiling water (*bain marie*) until thick, creamy and white, then gradually beat in the babaco and gelatine mixture.

5 Whisk in the remaining babaco pulp, stir until cool and almost set.

6 Whisk the egg whites until stiff, gently fold into the mixture. Pour into a suitable dish or dishes and chill for 2 hours in a refrigerator.

7 Decorate with glacé cherries and angelica. Serve with savoy fingers.

Note: Some babaco pieces can be placed in the bottom of the dish before the mixture is poured in.

BABACO FOOL

PREPARATION TIME: *40 minutes*   **COOKING TIME:** *10 minutes*   [M]

Ingredients *(per 4–6 persons)*:

400 g (1 lb) **Guernsey babaco**
100 g (4 oz) castor sugar
25 g (1 oz) cornflour
25 ml (1 fl oz) water
200 ml (8 fl oz) double cream
2 egg whites
25 g (1 oz) castor sugar

Method:

1 Cut the babaco into pieces and liquidise. Place in a saucepan together with the sugar and bring to the boil.

2 Slake the cornflour with the water and add to the boiling babaco pulp. Simmer for 1 minute, remove from the heat and allow to cool.

3 Whip the cream to a piping consistency. Save one-fifth for decoration and fold the rest into the babaco mixture.

4 Whisk one of the egg whites in a grease-free bowl to a stiff peak and gently fold into the mixture.

5 Pour into frosted glasses (dip the rims in the other egg white and then into castor sugar). Allow to set. Pipe a rosette of cream on top.

6 Serve with Biscuits à la Cuiller [savoy (sponge) fingers].

PETIT POT À LA CRÈME HAUTEVILLE

PREPARATION TIME: *30 minutes*

Ingredients *(per 4 persons)*:

200 g (8 oz) unsalted cream
   cheese
250 ml (½ pt) double cream
25 g (1 oz) castor sugar
2 egg whites
400 g (1 lb) **Guernsey babaco**
125 ml (¼ pt) single cream

Method:

1   Rub the cheese through a
fine sieve, mix with the lightly
whipped double cream and then
add the sugar.
2   Select some small round
plastic tubs and perforate the
bases to allow for drainage. Line
each pot with muslin (to ease
removal).
3   Whisk the egg whites and
gently fold them into the
mixture. Spoon the mixture into
the pots and place in a
refrigerator for 12 hours to drain

(stand the pots on a wire rack
and tray to ease draining).
4   Cut the babaco in half
lengthways and then into 1 cm
(⅓ in) slices.
5   Arrange the slices of babaco
neatly on sweet plates and turn
out the pots onto the centre of
the babaco (removing the
muslin).
6   Serve with the single cream,
which can be flavoured with a
little liqueur.

Note: Special moulds can be
purchased for this style of sweet.
They come in various shapes
and sizes and are already
perforated.

If cream cheese is not available
then cottage cheese can be used
but it does not give such a light
texture.

RUM AND RAISIN BABACO

PREPARATION TIME: *20 minutes*

Ingredients *(per 2 persons):*

75 g (3 oz) raisins
25 ml (1 fl oz) dark rum
200 g (8 oz) **Guernsey babaco**
125 ml (¼ pt) double cream
25 g (1 oz) castor sugar
125 ml (¼ pt) vanilla ice cream
2 crystallised violets
2 pompadour wafers

Method:

1 Roughly chop the raisins.
2 Soak the raisins in the rum until most of it has been absorbed.

3 Cut the babaco in half and then into thin slices.
4 Whip the cream with the sugar until stiff and fold in the raisins and any remaining rum. Chill in the refrigerator.
5 Line 2 coupe dishes with the sliced babaco and place a scoop of vanilla ice cream in the centre.
6 Spoon the rum and raisin cream around the ice cream and serve with a crystallised violet and pompadour wafer.

ICE CREAM-STUFFED BABACO BOAT

PREPARATION TIME: *20 minutes*

Ingredients *(per 4–6 persons)*:

1 800 g (2 lb) **Guernsey babaco**
25 ml (1 fl oz) Cointreau
25 g (1 oz) flaked almonds
500 ml (1 pt) coffee ice cream

Method:

1 Cut the babaco lengthways so that one of the halves will sit square on a serving dish (one of the five sides makes a flat base).
2 Scoop out the soft central pulp from the half used for the base. Place the base in the refrigerator to chill.
3 Slice the remaining half into 5 mm (¼ in) slices, sprinkle

with the Cointreau and chill in the refrigerator.

4 Toast the flaked almonds under the top grill until golden brown.

5 *To serve:* fill the centre cavity of the base half with the cold cold toasted flaked almonds and top with the ice cream so that it is heaped to a peak.

6 Cover the ice cream neatly with the babaco slices and serve immediately in thick slices.

BABACO MELBA

PREPARATION TIME: *15 minutes* **COOKING TIME:** *5 minutes*

Ingredients *(per 2 persons)*:

150 g (6 oz) **Guernsey babaco**
50 g (2 oz) raspberries
50 ml (2 fl oz) water
25 g (1 oz) castor sugar
10 g (⅓ oz) arrowroot
50 ml (2 fl oz) double cream
15 g (½ oz) flaked almonds
100 ml (4 fl oz) vanilla ice cream
2 pompadour wafer biscuits

Method:

1 Cut the babaco in half and then into 1 cm (⅓ in) slices. Place into 2 coupe dishes.

2 Liquidise the raspberries with the water, then strain through a fine sieve to remove the seeds.

3 Place the raspberry purée on to boil, add the sugar and thicken with the arrowroot which has been slaked with a little cold water. Reboil and allow to cool.

4 Whip the cream and toast the almonds under the top grill.

5 *To serve:* place a scoop of ice cream on top of the babaco, pipe the cream around the edge of the ice cream. Pour the melba sauce on top and sprinkle with the toasted flaked almonds. Decorate with a pompadour wafer.

BABACO ICE CREAM

PREPARATION TIME: *45 minutes*   **COOKING TIME:** *15 minutes*

Ingredients *(per 8 persons)*:

200 g (8 oz) **Guernsey babaco**
5 egg yolks
100 g (4 oz) castor sugar
150 ml (6 fl oz) full cream milk
125 ml (¼ pt) double cream

Method:

1 Cut the babaco into pieces and liquidise [to make 200 ml (8 fl oz)].
2 Whisk the egg yolks and sugar together until creamy and white.
3 Bring the milk to the boil and whisk in the egg yolk mixture (in a thick-bottomed pan). Return to a low heat and stir continuously with a wooden spatula until the mixture coats the back of a spoon.
4 Remove from the heat, whisk in the babaco pulp and pass through a fine strainer.
5 Cool, then freeze in an ice-cream machine, or in a freezer compartment, gradually adding the lightly whipped cream.

Note: 25 ml (1 fl oz) of Cointreau can be added to the mixture with the babaco pulp if required.

BABACO WATER ICE

PREPARATION TIME: *2–3 hours*   **COOKING TIME:** *10 minutes*

Ingredients *(per 4 persons)*:

100 g (4 oz) castor sugar
250 ml (½ pt) water
3 pieces orange zest
3 pieces lemon zest
1 teaspoon lemon juice
250 ml (½ pt) **Guernsey babaco**
    juice
2 egg whites

Method:

1 Dissolve the sugar in the water, bring to the boil and simmer for 10 minutes with the orange and lemon zest. Remove from the heat and stand for 15 minutes.
2 Strain, add the lemon juice and the babaco.

3 When cool, place in the refrigerator and freeze until it starts to turn mushy (stir the mixture regularly to prevent large crystals forming).
4 When crystals start to form whisk the egg whites and fold into the mixture. Freeze completely and serve as a sorbet or sweet.

Note: Half the water may be omitted and, after the liquid has been removed from the heat and cooled, the missing half substituted by Champagne (or sparkling wine).

BABACO YOGURT

PREPARATION TIME: *30 minutes*

Ingredients *(per 2 persons)*:

250 ml (½ pt) plain yogurt
150 g (6 oz) **Guernsey babaco**
25 g (1 oz) castor sugar

Method:

1 Either produce the yogurt with the aid of a yogurt maker as per instructions supplied with the unit or obtain ready-made commercial plain (un-flavoured) yogurt.

2 Cut the babaco into 1 cm (⅓ in) slices, peel, cut into 1 cm (⅓ in) cubes, place into a fine sieve and allow to drain for 15 minutes.
3 Squeeze the peel, collect the juice and dissolve the sugar in the juice.
4 Add the babaco cubes to the yogurt and sweeten to taste with the juice, being careful not to make the yogurt too liquid.

Preserves

BABACO BUTTER

PREPARATION TIME: *30 minutes* **COOKING TIME:** *45 minutes*

Ingredients:

200 g (8 oz) apples
1 kg (2½ lb) **Guernsey babaco**
250 ml (½ pt) cider
Granulated sugar
1 teaspoon cinnamon
1 teaspoon allspice

Method:

1 Wash and cut the apples into pieces (peel, core and pips included).
2 Cut the babaco into pieces and liquidise.
3 Place babaco, apples and cider in a pan, bring to the boil and simmer until apples are cooked. Pass the whole mixture through a fine sieve.
4 Measure, and to each 250 ml (½ pt) of liquid add 100 g (4 oz) granulated sugar.
5 Add the spices, place in a thick-bottomed pan, bring to the boil and boil until it thickens. To test, place a little onto a cold saucer and when cool, run a finger over the surface. If it wrinkles then the butter is ready. If not, boil a little longer.
6 Pour into clean, warmed, sterile jars and cover with waxed paper and cellophane.
7 Use like jam. Makes 1½ kg (4 lb).

BABACO CHUTNEY

PREPARATION TIME: *30 minutes*   **COOKING TIME:** *1½ hours*

Ingredients:

1½ kg (4 lb) **Guernsey babaco**
200 g (8 oz) apples, peeled and
  cored
2 green tomatoes
200 g (8 oz) shallots, chopped
200 g (8 oz) sultanas
200 g (8 oz) demerara sugar
75 cl (1½ pt) malt vinegar
2.5 cm (1 in) ginger root (dried)
12 peppercorns

Method:

1   Peel the babaco and cut the
flesh into cubes. Squeeze the
skin and save the juice.
2   Place the diced apples,
tomatoes, shallots, babaco,
sultanas and sugar into a thick-
bottomed pan.
3   Add the vinegar, babaco
juice and bring to the boil.
4   Place the ginger and
peppercorns into a muslin bag,
tie with string and place in the
pan.
5   Simmer until it reaches a
thick consistency with no excess
liquid.
6   Pour into sterile pots while
still hot. Cover with waxed
paper and cellophane.

Note: Makes approximately
1½ kg (4 lb).

BABACO CURD

PREPARATION TIME: *15 minutes*   **COOKING TIME:** *45 minutes*

Ingredients:

300 g (12 oz) **Guernsey babaco**
4 (size 3) eggs
25 ml (1 fl oz) lemon juice
100 g (4 oz) butter
400 g (1 lb) granulated sugar

Method:

1   Peel the babaco and liquidise
the flesh. Squeeze the skin and
add the juice to the pulp.
2   Place the babaco flesh,
beaten eggs, lemon juice, butter
and sugar in a bowl and stand

on a pan of boiling water (*bain-marie*).

3 Stir gently until the sugar has dissolved and the mixture thickens.

4 Sterilise some small pots in hot water, pour in the hot curd and cover with waxed paper and cellophane.

5 The curd will keep in a cool place for approximately 3–4 weeks. Makes 600 g (1½ lb).

BABACO AND APPLE JAM

PREPARATION TIME: *30 minutes*   **COOKING TIME:** *1½ hours*

Ingredients:

1½ kg (4 lb) **Guernsey babaco**
250 ml (½ pt) water
400 g (1 lb) dessert apple,
    peeled and cored
1 large lemon
1½ kg (4 lb) granulated sugar

Method:

1 Peel the babaco and cut the flesh into small cubes. Squeeze out the juice from the skin. Add to the water.

2 Cut the apple into pieces, put into a pan with water, babaco juice, lemon juice and zest. Cook the apple until soft.

3 Remove the lemon zest and pulp the apple to a purée.

4 Add the babaco and sugar to the apple, bring to the boil and simmer until a setting point is reached. (*To test:* place a little of the jam on a saucer, allow to cool then push finger along the surface. If it wrinkles then it is ready.)

5 Place in sterile pots and cover with waxed paper and cellophane tops.

Note: The setting test can also be done using a thermometer. Setting point is reached at 105°C.

Makes approximately 2½ kg (6 lb) jam.

BABACO JAM

PREPARATION TIME: *20 minutes*   **COOKING TIME:** *30 minutes*

Ingredients:

1 kg (2½ lb) **Guernsey babaco**
1 kg (2½ lb) granulated sugar
200 ml (8 fl oz) pectin

Method:

1 Cut the babaco into 1.5 cm (½ in) cubes.
2 Place the babaco, sugar and pectin in a thick-bottomed pan, bring to the boil and simmer for 15 minutes.
3 Check to see if setting point is reached by putting a little jam on a cold saucer, allow to cool then push finger along the surface. If the jam wrinkles then it is ready. If not set, return to the boil and check for the setting point regularly.
4 Once setting point is reached pour into sterile pots and cover with waxed paper and cellophane tops.

Note: The setting test can also be done using a thermometer. Setting point is reached at 105°C.

Makes approximately 1½ kg (4 lb) jam.

Recipe supplied by Roger Goodlass

Wines, Liqueurs & Cocktails

BABACO AND CIDER CUP

PREPARATION TIME: *15 minutes*

Ingredients *(per 10–12 persons)*:

400 g (1 lb) **Guernsey babaco**
1 orange
1 lemon
12 maraschino cherries
50 ml (2 fl oz) Calvados
1 litre (2 pt) dry sparkling cider, iced
250 ml (½ pt) tonic water
25 ml (1 fl oz) Grenadine
4 sprigs mint
12 ice cubes

Method:

1   Cut 12 thin half slices from the babaco and liquidise the remainder.

2   Pass the babaco pulp through a fine sieve.

3   Cut the orange and lemon into halves and slice thinly (remove any pips).

4   Place the babaco, orange and lemon slices and cherries in a large punch bowl, add the Calvados and 12 ice cubes.

5   *To serve:* add the iced cider, tonic water and Grenadine.

6   Stir, decorate with the mint and serve in ice-filled highball glasses with straws.

BABACO ELIXIR

PREPARATION TIME: *10 minutes*

Ingredients *(per 2 persons)*:

100 g (4 oz) **Guernsey babaco**
50 ml (2 fl oz) Bénédictine
4 dashes Angostura bitters
15 ml (½ fl oz) lime juice
15 ml (½ fl oz) sugar syrup
75 ml (3 fl oz) Perrier water

Method:

1 Liquidise the babaco and pass the juice through a fine sieve.

2 Place the babaco juice, Bénédictine, bitters, lime juice and sugar syrup [25 g (1 oz) sugar and 25 ml (1 fl oz) water boiled together for 1 minute and cooled] into an ice-filled shaker and shake well.
3 Strain into a highball glass and top with Perrier water. Dress with a slice of lime and serve with straws.

BABACO FIZZ

PREPARATION TIME: *5 minutes*

Ingredients *(per person)*:

100 g (4 oz) **Guernsey babaco**
25 ml (1 fl oz) cognac brandy
2 dashes sugar syrup.
50 ml (2 fl oz) champagne (or other dry sparkling wine)
1 sprig fresh mint

Method:

1 Peel the babaco and liquidise the flesh. Squeeze the peel and save the juice.
2 Stir over ice with the brandy and sugar syrup (see BABACO ELIXIR).
3 Strain into a flute glass, top with the Champagne (or other sparkling wine), lightly stir and serve dressed with the sprig of mint.

BABACO GIN SLING

PREPARATION TIME: *5 minutes*

Ingredients *(per person)*:

50 ml (2 fl oz) **Guernsey babaco** juice
½ teaspoon powdered sugar
½ teaspoon water
15 ml (½ fl oz) lemon juice
25 ml (1 fl oz) dry gin
2 ice cubes
1 lemon peel spiral

Method:

1 Strain the babaco juice through a fine strainer.
2 Dissolve the sugar in the water and lemon juice.
3 Pour all the ingredients into an old-fashioned glass or tumbler with 2 ice cubes.
4 Stir, add a spiral of lemon peel and serve.

BABACO LIQUEUR

PREPARATION TIME: *2 hours*   **COOKING TIME:** *15 minutes*

Ingredients *(per 1 litre [2 pt])*:

1 medium orange
1 kg (2½ lb) **Guernsey babaco**.
400 g (1 lb) sugar.
250 ml (½ pt) vodka

Method:

1 Remove the zest from the orange.
2 Liquidise the babaco, place in a pan and bring to the boil with the sugar and orange zest. Simmer for 15 minutes, removing any scum that forms.
3 Cover, remove from the heat and allow to cool. Strain through a sterile muslin bag or cloth, add the vodka.
4 Sterilise suitable bottles, fill with the liqueur and seal.
5 Allow to mature for at least 1 month.

BABACO PIPPIN

PREPARATION TIME: *5 minutes*

Ingredients *(per person):*

100 g (4 oz) **Guernsey babaco**
50 ml (2 fl oz) apple juice
75 ml (3 fl oz) soda water
1 slice of apple

Method:

1 Peel the babaco and liquidise the flesh with the apple juice and the juice from the skin.
2 Stir over ice in a highball glass.
3 Top with a splash of soda water, stir and serve with a slice of apple.

BABACO TIFFANY

PREPARATION TIME: *5 minutes*

Ingredients *(per person)*:

100 g (4 oz) **Guernsey babaco**
25 ml (1 fl oz) grapefruit juice
25 ml (1 fl oz) Lucozade

Method:

1 Peel the babaco and liquidise the flesh with the juice from the skin and the grapefruit juice.
2 Stir over ice in a highball glass.
3 Top with the Lucozade, stir and serve.

BABACO WINE

PREPARATION TIME: *45 minutes*

Ingredients *(per 4.5 litres [8 pt])*:

2 kg (5 lb) **Guernsey babaco**
2 medium oranges

2 lemons
15 g (½ oz) root ginger.

2 litres (4 pt) boiling water
1¼ kg (3 lb) sugar
15 g (½ oz) yeast.
Yeast nutrient

Method:

1 Liquidise the babaco and place in a clean, sterile bucket (or crock).
2 Slice the oranges and lemons, bruise the ginger and add to the babaco pulp.
3 Add the boiling water [sufficient to make a total volume of 4.5 litres (8 pt)] and 100 g (4 oz) of the sugar and allow to cool.
4 Add the yeast and yeast nutrient, cover and allow to ferment for 5–6 days, stirring frequently.
5 Strain into a clean, sterile

fermentation jar, dissolve the remaining sugar, fit an air-lock and allow to ferment out naturally.
6 When clear, syphon off the yeast sediment and bottle.

Note: This wine recipe should be produced under the usual home-made wine-making rules. If the wine does not clear naturally then a fining agent should be used.

Don't rush babaco wine by filtering too early or you will lose some of the delicate babaco perfume.

Ideally a dry wine but a sweet version (adding more sugar) is just as delicious.

Produces 6 bottles.

BREAKFAST BABACO CUP

PREPARATION TIME: *15 minutes*

Ingredients *(per 12 persons)*:

800 g (2 lb) **Guernsey babaco**
500 ml (1 pt) apple juice
100 ml (4 fl oz) grapefruit juice
50 ml (2 fl oz) orange juice
1 litre (2 pt) soda water
1 dessert apple, sliced
1 orange, sliced

Method:

1 Peel the babaco and liquidise the flesh.
2 Squeeze the skin, collect any juices and add to the babaco pulp.
3 Blend the babaco pulp with the other fruit juices and chill in the refrigerator.

4 Prior to serving add the iced soda water and sliced fruit.

5 Serve in highball glasses over ice.

CHÉRIE COCKTAIL

PREPARATION TIME: *5 minutes*

Ingredients *(per person)*:

50 ml (2 fl oz) **Guernsey babaco**
25 ml (1 fl oz) cherry brandy
15 ml (½ fl oz) maraschino
75 ml (3 fl oz) lemonade
1 maraschino cherry

Method:

1 Strain the babaco pulp through a fine strainer.
2 Stir the babaco juice, cherry brandy and maraschino over ice in a mixing jug.
3 Strain into an ice-filled highball glass. Top with lemonade and a maraschino cherry.

FRUIT CUP EXOTICA

PREPARATION TIME: *15 minutes*

Ingredients *(per 12 portions)*:

1 bottle sparkling (dry) wine
1 bottle lemonade
800 g (2 lb) **Guernsey babaco**
100 ml (4 fl oz) water
100 g (4 oz) sugar
125 ml (¼ pt) Cointreau
50 ml (2 fl oz) Kibowi liqueur
2 oranges (juice of)
4 small kiwi fruit
6 ice cubes

Method:

1 Chill the sparkling wine and lemonade.
2 Peel the babaco, saving any juices, squeeze the skin and save the juice. Place the skin with the water and sugar in a pan, bring to the boil and simmer for 5 minutes. Strain and allow to cool.
3 Blend the babaco flesh well in a liquidiser [saving 100 g

(4 oz) for the garnish] and strain into a punch bowl. Add the liqueurs, cold sugar syrup and orange juice.
4 Slice the remaining babaco and peeled kiwi fruit and place in a punch bowl.
5 When required add the wine, lemonade and 6 ice cubes. Serve in tall glasses with ice and straws.

HOT BABACO NOGGIN

PREPARATION TIME: *5 minutes* **COOKING TIME:** *5 minutes* **[M]**

Ingredients *(per person)*:

100 g (4 oz) **Guernsey babaco**
25 g (1 oz) castor sugar
40 ml (1½ fl oz) Jamaica rum
15 g (½ oz) unsalted butter
1 pinch nutmeg

Method:

1 Peel the babaco and liquidise the flesh. Squeeze the skin and collect any juices.
2 Gently heat the babaco purée over a low flame until almost boiling. Add the sugar and dissolve.
3 Place the dark rum in a warmed mug, add the babaco purée and stir well.
4 Float the butter on top and sprinkle with grated nutmeg. Serve with a spoon.

Note: Other spirits (whisky, brandy, etc) or port may be used in place of the rum. If too thick add a little boiling water.

KENILWORTH KISS

PREPARATION TIME: *5 minutes*

Ingredients *(per person)*:

25 ml (1 fl oz) **Guernsey babaco**
   juice
25 ml (1 fl oz) vodka
5 ml (¼ fl oz) lemon barley
   water
100 ml (4 fl oz) Perrier water
1 mint sprig.

Method:

1   Place the babaco juice, vodka and lemon barley water in a blender together with a scoop of crushed ice.

2   Blend well and strain into an ice-filled highball glass. Top with Perrier water and a mint sprig. Serve with straws.

KENILWORTH KOCKTAIL

PREPARATION TIME: *5 minutes*

Ingredients *(per person)*:

100 g (4 oz) **Guernsey babaco**
25 ml (1 fl oz) Kibowi liqueur
75 ml (3 fl oz) tonic water
1 slice kiwi fruit

Method:

1   Peel the babaco and purée in a blender.

2   Strain into a cocktail shaker, add Kibowi liqueur and ice cubes. Shake well, strain into a highball glass.

3   Top with tonic water and decorate with a slice of kiwi fruit.

MORNING GLORY

PREPARATION TIME: *10 minues*

Ingredients *(per 2 persons)*:

150 g (6 oz) **Guernsey babaco**
100 ml (4 fl oz) plain yogurt
1 scoop crushed ice
1 large egg white
25 ml (1 fl oz) lime juice cordial
15 g (½ oz) castor sugar
50 ml (2 fl oz) milk, iced
1 lime, sliced

Method:

1   Peel the babaco and liquidise the flesh. Squeeze the peel and save the juice.

2   Add the yogurt, ice, most of the egg white and lime juice cordial and blend well together.

3   Pour into frosted highball glasses (rims dipped in egg white and then in castor sugar), top with the iced milk.

4 Serve with a roundel of lime over the glass rim and straws.

SOUTH AMERICAN SHAKE

PREPARATION TIME: *5 minutes*

Ingredients *(per person):*

100 g (4 oz) **Guernsey babaco**
½ small egg white
1 dash grenadine
15 ml (½ fl oz) lime juice
25 ml (1 fl oz) tequila
75 ml (3 fl oz) lemonade
1 lime slice

Method:

1 Peel and liquidise the babaco, squeeze the skin and save the juice.
2 Shake the babaco purée, egg white, grenadine, lime juice and tequila well over ice.
3 Strain into a highball glass, top with lemonade. Serve with a slice of lime and straws.

TUTTI FRUTTI COCKTAIL

PREPARATION TIME: *5 minutes*

Ingredients *(per person):*

1 scoop crushed ice
50 ml (2 fl oz) **Guernsey babaco** pulp
25 ml (1 fl oz) cognac brandy
15 ml (½ fl oz) crème de fraises
75 ml (3 fl oz) soda water
1 fresh strawberry/maraschino cherry

Method:

1 Blend the crushed ice, babaco pulp, brandy and crème de fraises together in a blender.
2 Pour into a highball glass.
3 Top with soda water.
4 Serve with a fresh strawberry (when in season) or a cherry and straws.

Acknowledgements

To produce any book a great deal of help is usually required and *The Guernsey Babaco Cook Book* is no exception.

Special thanks must go to the first commercial Guernsey babaco growers: John Langlois, Harold Dally, John Davis, Jeff Gillingham and Nick Carey who have taken so much care in producing this remarkable fruit and have made the fruit available for us to cook with and so compile this book.

Also to the members of the Guernsey States Horticultural Advisory Service for their invaluable assistance and information. Especially to the Director, David Miller, who introduced the babaco to Guernsey and to John Ogier, the group's technical leader.

To Ariel Shai, an exotic fruit expert with a world-wide reputation, whose guidance and enthusiasm has inspired the growers.

To Ken James and his family for their untiring help and support and finally to all those who have contributed and tested the recipes included in this book.

Recipe Index

Andian Potatoes [M] [V], 86
Babaco and Almond Cloud, 121
Babaco and Apple Jam, 146
Babaco and Apple Pie, 97
Babaco and Apple Slice, 104
Babaco and Carrot Salad [V], 88
Babaco and Carrot Soup [M] [V], 3
Babaco and Cider Cup, 148
Babaco and Frangipane Bake [M], 117
Babaco and Herb Soup [V], 4
Babaco and Kiwi Jelly, 134
Babaco and Lamb Rissoles, 43
Babaco and Mussel Salad, 8
Babaco and Raisin Bread [M], 110
Babaco and Turkey Casserole [M], 62
Babaco and Walnut Salad [V], 94
Babaco and Watercress Salad [V], 90
Babaco Baked Egg Italienne [V], 5
Babaco Betty, 106
Babaco Bisque, 4
Babaco Bordelaise [M], 124
Babaco Brazilian [M], 136
Babaco Brûlée, 106
Babaco Butter, 144
Babaco Cambrai, 107
Babaco Cheesecake, 109
Babaco Cheese Fondue [V], 66
Babaco Chutney, 145
Babaco Citron [V], 92
Babaco Clafoutis [V], 68
Babaco Crêpes Rue des Prés, 115
Babaco Crumble [M], 107
Babaco Curd, 145
Babaco Cushions, 118
Babaco Dressing [V], 88
Babaco Egg Timbale [V], 6
Babaco Elixir, 148
Babaco En Papillote [M], 123
Babaco Farci aux Amandes, 131
Babaco Fermière [M], 38
Babaco Fingers with Pernod Sauce, 124
Babaco Fish Bake [M], 19

Babaco Fizz, 149
Babaco Flan, 96
Babaco Florentine [V], 69
Babaco Fool [M], 138
Babaco French Style, 139
Babaco Fritters, 104
Babaco Gin Sling, 149
Babaco Hors d'Oeuvres, 8
Babaco Ice Cream, 142
Babaco in Red Wine [M], 125
Babaco in Tarragon Cream [V], 14
Babaco Jam, 147
Babaco Jonathon [M], 108
Babaco Kebabs la Poidevine, 55
Babaco la Bellengere [M] [V], 69
Babaco les Plichons, 122
Babaco Liqueur, 150
Babacomango, 134
Babaco Meat Marinade, 38
Babaco Melba, 141
Babaco Midfield [V], 77
Babaco Mill Lane [M], 56
Babaco Nut Crunch [M] [V], 65
Babaco Pippin, 151
Babaco Polonaise [M] [V], 66
Babaco Provençale [M] [V], 70
Babaco Rice Pudding [M], 117
Babaco Rumtopf, 135
Babaco Salad with Herb Yogurt Dressing
  [V], 95
Babaco Snow, 137
Babaco Soufflé, 132
Babaco Stroganoff [M] [V], 81
Babaco Strudel, 100
Babaco-Stuffed Tomatoes [M] [V], 85
Babaco Surprise, 128
Babaco Tagliatelle, 50
Babaco Tiffany, 151
Babaco Upside-Down Pudding [M], 102
Babaco Victor Hugo, 110
Babaco Water Ice, 142
Babaco Wine, 151

Babaco with Cream Cheese and Herbs [V], 94
Babaco Yogurt, 143
Bacon and Babaco Casserole [M], 48
Baked Babaco Creole [M] [V], 85
Baked Babaco-Stuffed Apple [M], 119
Baked Babaco with Crab [M], 24
Baked Halibut Sarnia [M], 25
Baked Mackerel with Babaco Sauce [M], 27
Baked Stuffed Babaco [M], 114
Bateau de Babaco aux Fruits d'été, 131
Beefy Babaco Boats [M], 39
Braised Ham Prince Albert [M], 49
Braised Rabbit with Babaco Marinade [M], 63
Breakfast Babaco Cup, 152
Calf's Liver Guernsey Style [M], 53
Caviar-Stuffed Babaco, 9
Celtic Torte, 101
Chérie Cocktail, 153
Chicken in Mustard Sauce [M], 57
Christmas Babaco [M], 111
Cocktail Babaco Fruits de Mer, 10
Congre Grandes Rocques [M], 23
Coquilles Saint Jacques Torteval, 33
Corn-on-the-Cob with Babaco Dressing [M] [V], 15
Coupe Babaco à la Menthe [V], 16
Curried Babaco Grande Mare [M] [V], 71
Curried Babaco with Prawns [M], 31
Devilled Babaco [V], 17
Eastern Pork [M], 45
Edwardian Chicken [M], 57
Exotic Fruits Guernsey Style, 129
Filets de Sole Carica [M], 36
Fish in Babaco and Green Herb Sauce [M], 20
Fricassé of Monkfish with Babaco and Ginger [M], 28
Fried Skate with Babaco and Sage Sauce [M], 24
Frogs' Legs with Babaco Sauce [M], 35
Fruit Cup Exotica, 153
Ginger Babaco Bake [M], 103
Ginger Babaco with Crispy Seaweed [V], 82
Grilled Gammon and Babaco [M], 51
Guernsey Babaco Fish Chowder [M], 21
Guernsey Babaco Tart [M], 98

Guernsey Burger, 40
Guernsey Coleslaw [V], 90
Guernsey Muesli [V], 1
Guernsey Platter [V], 12
Guernsey Trifle, 126
Guernsey Veal Olives [M], 51
Haddock and Babaco Toasties [M], 79
Ham and Babaco Savouries, 80
Ham Cornets [M], 11
Hot Babaco Noggin [M], 154
Hot Babaco Soufflé, 116
Ice Cream-Stuffed Babaco Boat, 140
Island Bounty, 137
Island Chicken [M], 58
Island Pudding [M], 103
Kenilworth Kiss, 154
Kenilworth Kocktail, 155
Lamb Cutlets Heilborn [M], 43
Leeks with Babaco Cream Sauce [M] [V], 84
Lettuce Savouries [M] [V], 80
Lobster with Babaco Cream Sauce [M], 26
Malted Babaco [M], 112
Mama's Canneloni [M] [V], 75
Maraschino Babaco [M], 133
Marinated Babaco with Mint Yogurt [V], 96
Marinated Eel [M], 10
Meat Balls in Spicy Babaco Sauce [M], 40
Morning Glory, 155
Mussel, Mushroom and Babaco Pie [M], 30
Mussels Island Style [M], 29
Oat Cocktail with Fruit [V], 1
Orange and Babaco Salad [V], 92
Oriental Salad [V], 91
Petit Pot à la Crème Hauteville, 139
Pheasant Suzanne [M], 62
Pimento la Saline [M] [V], 73
Pizza Babaco, 78
Poached Babaco with Sabayon Sauce [M], 119
Poisson la Ramée [M], 22
Red Cooked Chicken, 59
Rendezvous dans Paradis [M] [V], 72
Risotto Guernésiais [M] [V], 76
Roast Babaco-Stuffed Belly Pork, 46
Roast Beef Carey [M], 41
Rognons d'Agneau Sauté Lihou [M], 54
Rum and Raisin Babaco, 140
Saddle of Lamb with Glazed Babaco, 44

Salade Exotica [V], 93
Salmon Steak Saint Pierre [M], 31
Sark Salad, 13
Saumarez Charlotte, 127
Savoury Babaco Cake [M] [V], 67
Savoury Babaco Potato [M] [V], 87
Scampis Moulin Huet [M], 33
Soused Babaco Herrings [M], 26
South American Duck [M], 61
South American Shake, 156
Southern Babaco Pie, 99
Spicy Babaco Beef [M], 42
Spicy Babaco Eggs [V], 7
Stewed Babaco [M], 112
Stuffed Sea Bream with Babaco and Almonds [M], 34
Summer Babaco Pudding, 127
Suprëme of Salmon with Dill Babaco [M], 32

Sweet Babaco Kebabs, 120
Sweet Braised Pork [M], 48
Sweet-n-Sour Pork with Babaco, 47
Sweet Omelette Exotica, 122
Tangy Island Surprise [V], 17
Tipsy Babaco, 133
Treasure Trove, 83
Tropical Curried Chicken Salad, 60
Turbot and Babaco Mousse with Orange Sauce, 36
Tutti Frutti Cocktail, 156
Veal Escalope Roncefer, 52
Vegetarian Pillows [M] [V], 73
West Coast Pie [V], 74
Westwood Babaco, 13
Yuletide Salad [V], 88